The Vantage Chronicles

A business book with a difference

Real stories of success, failure and everything in between,
from entrepreneurs you can relate to

Ben Reynolds & Henry Kay

Vantage Network

Printed in Great Britain

Remus House, Coltsfoot Drive, Peterborough, PE2 9BF

ISBN 978-1-913284-27-5

Ben and Henry would like to take this opportunity to thank our wives, Sarah and Sam, for putting up with us whilst we have created this book, and for supporting our various entrepreneurial ideas over the years.

We also want to thank all of those who have helped us on the way with introductions, advice and words of encouragement. It really does mean the world to us both and we are lucky to have such an amazing network.

For Isabelle, Ella, Tilly and Alfie, we hope one day you will be able to point to this book somewhere in the world and be proud of who created it.

CONTENTS

FOREWORD

My name is James W Phillips and I am the owner of the JWP Group, based in the United Kingdom. My association with the authors of this valuable book goes back to early 2020 and I was honoured when asked to write the foreword. I thought, "what can I write that sets the scene for the insights to follow, and that gives value not only for the reader but also adds to book sales!"

After a few days pondering, I began to realise my journey as an entrepreneur like so many before me and those included in this book, has been one of huge highs, and huge lows, but of ultimate success. Want to know why and how? Well, those secrets are contained within. No one dreams of being an 'entrepreneur' when they are at school. It develops as a consequence of your ambitions and goals as you start to experience life, and the rewards that present themselves as a result; a better car, a nice watch, life experiences, freedom, time, surrounding yourself with beautiful people, and ultimately security, happiness and fulfilment - but also danger, risk and high stakes.

Becoming an entrepreneur is often sparked by a chance meeting or a consequence of something massive happening in your life. My path that I travelled was not an easy one, but truly helped me become the success I am today. What do I mean by success? It's not just about money! It's about your popularity and reputation. My father was a farmer, my mother a florist. When the life force that was my dad left this world, a bolt of lightning struck me within, and seven years on I have multiple business interests in the UK, the USA, Monaco and the French Riviera and party on yachts with beautiful people and through my foundation

I mentor high school children in New York. Sounds great, right? Behind the scenes there have been battles - mentally, physically, emotionally and legally - across two continents, while holding down a successful City job. That's why this book is such a breath of fresh air, it tells the real gritty stories behind the Champagne lifestyle because behind every sip of Champagne there lies a story of sacrifice, late nights, stress, worry, zero money in the bank, a chronic sense of imposter syndrome and lack of self-belief, and daily battles with other people's negativity. But countering that are huge highs, rewarding relationships with your peers, and when you are recognised and make some money, the joy you feel is like no other feeling you will ever experience.

Millions of people around the world start a business, and everyone has a dream to make their life better, however not all those that start a business succeed, and not all those who dream of a better life actually make any changes at all. They go through life in a very linear fashion, living day by day, trapped hanging onto a dream that they have no idea how to make a reality. That is why sustaining a life as an entrepreneur is a way of life, it consumes your life until you have 'made it' and not many do. Even then when you have spent your whole life and every last buck making it, the entrepreneur inside you will keep telling you to carry on, even when you have millions in the bank and you don't need to keep hustling. That is a true measure of an entrepreneur, you are never really satisfied, and you will always want more, climbing higher, achieving more and staying hungry.

Within this book you will read the rags-to-riches stories, the toils and successes and real-life true grit journeys of sacrifice from real entrepreneurs putting everything on the line, day after day. That's the standout element that makes this book feel so unique, it doesn't gloss over the reality or try to sell you a fantasy. If your dream is to sit on a superyacht on the Côte D'Azur surrounded by endless beauty with a glass of Champagne and want to know how to do it, then read on and find out how to really achieve your dream goals. I will meet you there!

James W Phillips - CEO JWP Group.

INTRODUCTION

BEN REYNOLDS

Firstly, before you get into this book I want to thank you for taking the time to read this section, and in fact for reading the book in its entirety. Please read and re-read this book to ensure you take away as much as possible from it. There is a lot of information and guidance included and our hope is you can use it as a tool to go on and do great things with your own journey.

This book was written out of a passion for everything entrepreneurial and the desire to build something outside of the normal 9-5. I hope that you get as much enjoyment and motivation from reading this book as Henry and I did in putting it together.

Entrepreneurship has always been part of my life. Whether this was watching my father work every hour God sent to make his businesses a success, or whether it was me and my older brother mending punctures on our friends' push bikes for whatever pennies they had as kids, I have always found the idea of being responsible for your own life and wellbeing fascinating.

The idea for this book came to me while working on one of my first businesses I owned along with a friend. I spent countless hours reading about these multi-millionaires or billionaires who had done amazing things but always found them difficult to relate to as they were so far past the current position me and my business were in. I wanted to read about people who were still growing their businesses, had recently started up, or were going through a stage of growth, people who I could somehow relate to. Of course, in this book you will read about international football players who you may struggle to relate to on a personal level, but will be able to relate to the challenges they face growing a side hustle whilst holding down a full time job.

This book, and the company Vantage Network, has been set up as a side-hustle. I am a firm believer in having an interest outside of your normal 9-5 and actually how having this can benefit you and your employer by adopting a "what if this was my business" approach to daily tasks.

I had been procrastinating about how to start this book and business and it was when I met Henry and bonded with him instantly that I knew we could make it a success. I loved his drive and the fact he had already started and was growing a successful business and could fill the gaps in my skill-set needed to get this off the ground. Throughout this process we have used our network and built our network in order to make sure we feature entrepreneurs who have a good story to tell. I encourage you to make sure you constantly look to grow your little black book of contacts and offer to help your network wherever and however you can as in my experience you really do get back what you put out there.

This book started as a passion project and it has been this passion that has kept us going. Henry and I have spent hours in virtual meetings, driven up and down the country to meet the entrepreneurs where possible, spent evenings and weekends pulling it all together and we hope that the final product reflects this. We have very understanding families and friends who have supported us and we hope that you take from this, and other stories in the book, that the entrepreneurial journey comes with having to make many sacrifices, and with no guarantees of success, but still despite this, the journey is one we want to do time and time again.

Thank you again for taking the time to pick this book as one of hopefully many you are going to read. If you enjoy it, we would love to hear from you. If you didn't, we would love to hear from you. Henry and I wish you the best of luck in your own journey, and if you only take one small bit of information, or motivation, from this book and it helps you build something you are proud of, then we have done our job.

HENRY KAY

When I first met Ben, at a regular day job that we'd both recently joined, we clicked immediately because I think we could sense that we were both entrepreneurial people, with far greater ambitions than just working for that company, or anyone else's. Like many people, trudging through an often stressful or boring 9-5 job has never sat comfortably with me.

We spoke more about our own business ventures than the actual job that we were starting! My first venture was when I had a random little idea in the gym one morning before work four years previously. After a workout, I would often refuel by reheating last night's leftovers, adding a squeeze of ketchup, or other tasty sauce, to bring it back to life. But then something stopped me. I realised that it didn't make sense to put all that effort in at the gym, and in preparing healthy meals, only to cover my food in salt, sugar and preservatives.

With absolutely zero experience in starting a business or creating a food product, I got cracking by researching for hours and hours online and playing around with ingredient ideas in the kitchen. My starting point was simply a blank Google Slides doc that I dumped all of my ideas, images and goals onto - a kind of mood board that I could access and add to anywhere on any device as it sat in the cloud.

After a discussion with my cousin Mark Webb (a successful entrepreneur in his own right, having used his passion for cars to set up 'Webbs of Weybridge' Classic Car Hire www.webbsofweybridge.co.uk), I shared my idea with a small group of local entrepreneurs in a village pub where they had begun meeting monthly to network and bounce around ideas. I returned each month, five or six times, with further developments on the idea. There was a guy called Nick Briggs there each time, who was really interested and excited about the potential and so we spoke further and decided that the world needed a new kind of ketchup – one that's perfect for foodies and fitness lovers – so we teamed up. Nick has been the driving force since day one and I definitely couldn't have created and released IN THE BUFF Protein Ketchups without him at the helm.

I'm really proud of what we have achieved so far, being listed on Amazon and Ocado initially, and we continue to work hard to try and grow the business as much as we can.

www.proteinketchup.co.uk @inthebuffsauce on social media.

I was really impressed by what Ben had achieved up to the point when we met and when he said that he had always wanted to bring out an inspiring and relatable business book I jumped at the chance to be part of making it happen.

Like with my food products, this was completely new territory - I'd never written a book before, but I knew that we could make it happen (as another side hustle alongside our necessary day jobs and busy young family lives) with sheer perseverance. I am really proud that you are now reading our words and hope that you enjoy the following amazing stories and advice, and close the book feeling inspired to make your crazy little idea into a reality.

Something that is definitely true is the power of networking - a case in point was going for a pint in that little Surrey pub and meeting my IN THE BUFF business partner Nick. This book also wouldn't have happened without some of the people that we know and we soon helped to create some new collaborations via introductions we made between some of the brilliant people in this book.

I really believe in the power of reading and knowledge - that's exactly what this book is about. I'll admit that I'm often exhausted by the day job, the kids and life in general, but I always end the day by reading a book or magazine in bed at night. Of course, sometimes I manage about three words before nodding off, but I do think that there is no limit to the amount of information you can absorb from books, so I love to read both business and fiction stories, to fuel my ambition.

We hope that once you've absorbed the incredible and inspiring stories in these pages that you will feel your own buzz of excitement, feel a little bit wiser and feel that you can rise up from your current position to one that is higher and more successful. Enjoy!

The Vantage Chronicles

CHAPTER 1

DANNY GRAY

Danny has already made a success out of a business that was born out of his personal body and mental health issues. It's difficult enough dealing with such feelings, so to create his business during that time and alongside a full-time day job is incredible. Making the decision to take the leap into turning a ten year idea into a business, with zero experience or knowledge of how to do it, takes balls. We are really excited about Danny's newest venture, which at the time of writing is only a few weeks away from launch - watch this space!

Tell us who you are and what you do:

My name is Danny Gray and I am the founder of War Paint For Men which I designed from the ground up specifically for a male audience to help break down the stereotypes of men wearing makeup.

What were you doing before you set up War Paint For Men?

Before I set up War Paint I was a salesperson in different sectors including audio but mostly automotive. As well as this I was doing a few things on the side like having a bouncy castle company when I was 16 which I sold after a year or two, and spent the money on travelling. I then started a car valeting business when I was 18, on the side as well, but mainly before War Paint it was quite corporate, although I think I have always been very entrepreneurial.

When you were employed was there a plan on how to get out and do your own thing?

Definitely. Wherever I worked I always wanted to progress and I would always come up with ideas to do things in a better way, whether it was how to streamline things or just ideas about the business. I always knew I was never going to be a long-term 9-5'er, which doesn't mean there is anything wrong with that, but I wanted to be the thought leader. I was always thinking about things I could do but nothing made me think "wow, this is the one, this is worth giving everything up for". I had lots of ideas, but none were scalable, until War Paint.

How did you get started?

I actually got started by taking a plunge on the golf course when my best mate told me to stop thinking about it and just do it. I have had my own mental health and body dysmorphia issues and have been wearing makeup for 20 years so I thought, fuck it, I'm going to do it. I sat in the golf club car park for four hours calling everyone I knew for advice on how to start a business and start a brand. I had no idea about anything, not about the website, product, nothing. I got started by using what little savings I had to buy some really cheap, crap makeup products and put stickers on them and then created a website off the back of that. I tested the market to see if there was demand - which I saw very quickly within five days. At this point I stopped everything as I knew in order to do it properly, I had to secure quite a large investment.

We got things set up online and started working with some e-tailers who gave me some feedback which I took on board. Once this was done, I had to find a manufacturer and after a lot of no's, having literally begged for a meeting, I got one and sold them the dream and thankfully they reduced their MOQ (Minimum Order Quantity). My first order was £92,000. Creating your own makeup is expensive. I had to re-mortgage my house, sell my car and sell my watches, and I got investment through a family member who took an equity stake in the business. It took about another five to six months to source all the packaging from China, contacts, labels of ingredients, etc. and then it launched in November 2018.

You mentioned you had several ideas for other businesses. What made War Paint the one you knew would work?

I had been thinking about it for ten years. It had always been the one I kept coming back to. I was always talking to people about it, about how a proper men's makeup brand that was edgy could really work. The market wasn't right and I wanted to see if anything else was coming into it, which is a risk, and I waited a long time. Even with the other business ideas, this one never went away.

What was the feedback from friends and family when you told them about your idea, and did you take any notice of it?

My family gave me 100 per cent backing which was amazing. Even though it was using up all the money I had, they said just go for it. That is very much my family's approach to a lot of things.

Some of my friends didn't necessarily try to talk me out of it but suggested a different style and making the makeup gender neutral effectively. I was almost swayed a couple of times but I stuck to my guns and just went with my plan.

What was the reason for sticking just with men's makeup?

It wasn't really to do with having a unique selling point or anything like that, it was because that's what I knew. I was the target demographic. It is what I had been talking about for ten years, although to this day I still get imposter syndrome thinking that this isn't going to work, or that I can't do it. When you doubt yourself and someone suggests doing it a different way you risk changing everything, but my gut was telling me that this is a male makeup brand.

What was the first priority you had?

The website. People think it's easy, but it's not. It's all about the content. We did videos, education, had to work on the brand and the messaging, that was really big for us. In November 2018 we built through social advertising.

Our first month we forecasted to do £2,000 and we actually did £11,000. Our second month, I forecasted £5,000, we did £28,000 and in the third we did £36,000. We did all of this from a little flat in Watford where I was packing the orders. That was great for about six weeks but then you look and when you've got 60 orders to do it's really hard. It grew really quickly and I've actually moved office nine times and we are only two years old, because we've outgrown them. We moved from my flat in Watford to an office, then moved to a bigger flat in the same building. Then we got a separate office just for stock but it was on a different floor, so I would have to keep going up to do the picking and packing then go to the post office which was downstairs and if I missed that, I would have to load up my fucking small car and drive it to Hermes down the road. It was fucking carnage. I was actually pissed off because we had so many orders as I didn't know anything about fulfilment!

What was the hardest part of setting up the business?

The hardest part was probably regulations, ingredients and things like that which I knew nothing about. That was really difficult. The finances were tough, I'm good with numbers but having to learn about P&L, margins, stock management, retail costs and things like that was tricky. I was setting up retail prices from the current costs not thinking about price changes when we order tens of thousands and things like that. There's so many different little things like that which you don't think about.

It was also difficult dealing with third parties like some of the agencies who promise you the world but actually do fuck all but cost you money. You learn a lot of shit on the job. I loved learning about everything, but when you start it does feel like around every corner there is something new that you have to learn.

Were there any points where you thought you had made a mistake in setting up on your own?

I still think that everyday at some point! Not so much that I've made a mistake but whether or not it will continue to work. When I started War Paint it was a side hustle for the first nine months whilst we built it and that was the best I've ever felt. It was the weirdest feeling knowing that I had something going on on the side that was all mine. Your job is your job, but I was waking up everyday thinking, "God, I've got my own business!" What a good fucking feeling that was, it was unbelievable.

How long did it take you to start making money?

It took us about 14 months before we actually started selling whilst we were creating the website, getting the products sorted, sorting shipping and all things like that. As I mentioned earlier, I had tested the market and sold £300 worth but before we really started selling it was 14 months.

This was only generating revenue, not making a profit though. I'm still not making a profit now and won't be for another two years. You have two options when it comes to business, you either have a growth business or a lifestyle business. I could quite easily just tick along and make this a lifestyle business, but we wouldn't have grown at the rate we have done with regards to the exposure, sales, team resource and everything just getting better. I have reinvested everything to grow the business.

As you are running it as a growth business, do you have an exit strategy?

I think if you are running a business just for a sale you run it in a very different way. I am VC (Venture Capitalist) backed and quite heavily now so everyone will have a strategy with their investment to some extent, but for me it's not about just growing it to sell it, I really want to make an impact with the brand. But that being said, if someone turned round and offered me £100 million today, I may think about it!

You went on *Dragons' Den,* how was that as an experience?

It was crazy. We had some mad shit happen the week before where we went viral, but in a negative way. We'd been on *ABC News* and *Good Morning America* and on the way up to do *Dragons' Den*, the *Huffington Post* called my mobile and I had to do an interview for them. It wasn't really a good interview, we talked about masculinity and what I had to say about it.

When I got to *Dragons' Den*, I was really nervous, but it actually went OK, well actually it went really well. We had all five Dragons make an offer and it was a really surreal experience. I hadn't realised, because of what had happened on the way up and the week before, how much pressure I had put on myself and when we got outside I just broke down. In the end, despite them offering lower equity after we had shot the interview, I turned them down. It was a great experience overall but I just didn't feel like it was the right time and then we went on to raise the money about six months later. We actually trended on social media afterwards with people saying I should negotiate Brexit! *The Daily Mail, The Sun* and others wrote about it the day after and then major retailers contacted me about stocking it. If it had gone wrong however, it could have killed the brand.

How long was it before you took on your first member of staff?

It was only about three weeks because I had started it part-time as a side hustle whilst I still had my job going and rather than outsourcing various parts I thought it was better to get an all-rounder type of person to come in and do it all. I hired a 19-year-old who was incredibly talented who could do a bit of everything.

I funded it out of my own money, and paid her well, and she was very talented and good at creating things. As someone who didn't know how to do this kind of thing, for me it was perfect. I did however make a mistake and asked her how much she wanted to be paid to which she turned it around and asked how much I wanted to pay her, which put the pressure on to make her a better offer than perhaps I should have done, but I have learned from it. I probably could have paid her half of what I paid her and we both would be happy.

What parts of the business, if any, did you outsource?

A lot was kept in-house between my first employee and me. Between us we could pretty much do anything, I was alright at the number side of things and she was good at being creative. The first thing we did outsource though was fulfilment and it literally changed the business overnight.

The owner of the fulfilment company came to speak to me and we talked about whether we could do it in-house but he then pointed out that I would have to pay that person anyway, and manage them, cover sick leave and picking mistakes and actually to know every order was going out correctly was worth it. My stocktake used to consist of counting boxes and when we got down to the last one I would order another lot and be told it was a 12 week wait. Fucking hell. I had a week's worth left and ran out of stock completely a couple of times. As soon as it was outsourced, there was a much better system in place.

Up until now, what has been the hardest and best year of business?

We've only really been going for three years but the hardest was the first year just because it was so full on, but also the six-month period when we were going through raising funds. The politics of it all was difficult with existing shareholders and then new shareholders and sometimes you feel like no-one really gives a shit about your view on your own business.

The best time was probably the last five months. The team has been built out, I have a lot more freedom to do what I want to do and I just love it.

What were your reasons for bringing on a Chairman to the business and do you think it's something every entrepreneur should look at?

100 per cent. You don't need one right from the start obviously, but to have someone there who is the overriding 'referee' can be priceless. The value he has shown me in the last two months alone has been priceless. As a founder you take on the stress of everything, but you shouldn't be dealing with the day to day, you need to go and build the brand and build the business. Before we had a Chairman I was working in Customer Services and he pointed out that our brand was too big for the founder to be working in that role. He introduced me to working *on* the business and not working *in* the business.

If you were to start up again today, what, if anything, would you do differently?

Absolutely nothing. I sometimes look at old pictures and think if I hadn't done some of the things I did back then I wouldn't be where I am today. If I knew then what I know now, would we have gotten the same traction as we got? No. Would we have gone viral even if it was for the wrong reasons? No. Would I have gone on *Dragons' Den*? No, probably not. I would have streamlined everything but wouldn't have made the same mistakes which have helped grow this brand.

How do you manage your time and ensure you have time for your family as well?

The first 18 months it was really tough and I think it would be for anyone in business. You have to give it fucking everything especially if you have another full-time job like I did.

Now, I am very strict and I work from 7.30 or 8 am till 5 pm when I go home and play with my kids, bath them and put them to bed and that's something I'm not going to give up. My reasoning for this is that my phone is on and if anything dramatic has happened someone will call me about it. You aren't going to get any further forward sending emails late at night as the other person won't be picking them up then to action them so there's no real point.

What are the most important qualities an entrepreneur should have?

There are so many different qualities for different types of people, but self-belief is a big one – which I don't really have. I think anyone can be an entrepreneur and use their skill sets for different things, a lot of it comes down to mindset.

What has been the most important lesson you have learnt so far?

Go with your gut. The two times I haven't done this, it has cost me a lot of time and a lot of money. Your gut is right 99 out of 100 times. Someone once told me that if you have an idea that you want to do in business, imagine you didn't and someone else did, and if it turns your stomach that you didn't do it, that's your gut telling you to go for it. If you don't get that feeling (of your stomach turning when thinking of someone else doing it), then you shouldn't. Trust your gut.

What does the next five years look like for you?

We've got a plan and strategy for where we want to get to with War Paint and I just want to enjoy that ride and make it as big as I can. I'm so proud to say that I've just opened my flagship retail store on Carnaby Street in London! The next five years for any business regardless of what stage they are at is going to be huge. For me, the main goal is to make my family proud, over everything. I want to be in a pub when I'm 60 and have someone ask me what I used to do, I tell them I started a men's makeup brand and they know it's War Paint.

Outside of War Paint, I am working on a new service aimed at helping individuals with mental health issues. I am launching JAAQ which stands for 'Just Ask A Question' and it is a first of its kind support service where users can ask industry experts and celebrities questions about everything to do with mental health including stress, anxiety, body dysmorphia and so much more. We have spent hours with experts asking them the questions people who are struggling want to know the answers to and they can use their phone or laptop and get the answer straight from the expert. It is going to revolutionise how people access support in real time and it is being set up as a not-for-profit. I'm not interested in making money out of this, as someone who has had mental health struggles in the past, I want to help as many people as I can on a global scale get the answers they need in order to help them.

What is your favourite entrepreneur quote?

If you're 70 per cent sure on something, go for it, because you'll never be 100 per cent certain. If you're 70 per cent sure you're probably on to something and it's better to try it at 70 per cent and fail than not try it at all.

If you weren't doing War Paint and JAAQ, what would you be doing?

Doing something I wouldn't be interested in, while thinking of an idea for a business to start.

Do you think there is a point in an entrepreneur's life when they feel like they have made it?

No. Let's say I sell War Paint and easily have enough money to retire, there is no way I am going to be sitting at home doing nothing. I will always be wanting to be doing something. It's not the finished product which is the best thing, it's the getting there. I don't think a true entrepreneur will ever say they have made it and stop.

Danny Gray - Warpaint for Men / JAAQ

Websites: warpaintformen.com / Jaaq.co.uk

Instagram: @warpaintformen / @dannygray_wpjq / jaaqofficial

Twitter: @warpaintformen / @dannygraywp

CHAPTER 2

TONY TROWERS

The story of Tony Trowers is such an inspiring one. Tony went from a 'humble plasterer' as he calls it, to a property empire, against the odds and because of his sheer determination to get there. This is another clear example of just how powerful tenacity and belief can be and how important it is to be like a sponge and educate yourself as much as possible. We all have access to books and the internet, so there is nothing stopping you from using your time wisely by learning about every single facet of your chosen business area. Tony has made a point of remaining down to earth and grateful for his success, having been around others who aren't like that, it's so nice to see and can only be a positive thing - business is a lot to do with how you sell yourself.

Can you tell us a little about your business ventures?

I suppose you would describe me as an entrepreneur and a serial investor these days but I started off as a humble plasterer with a burning ambition. My core business is property development and with a lot of hard work over 35 years I have established a multi-award-winning group of companies within the specialist trades and construction, property acquisition and management, sales and lettings agencies and financial services sectors.

Although Stoke on Trent is centric to my operations, and I have been dubbed 'Mr Staffordshire', I've worked throughout the UK and also have business interests in the United Arab Emirates, Qatar and the Middle East.

I founded 'Art Plastering Systems' in 1983. Because of my own perfectionism the company became known for its quality workmanship and professionalism and has been recognised nationally within the housing building sector as best in class. Whilst subcontracting I moved into property development and building an extensive property portfolio.

In the 2000s, I founded the 'Pillar Box Group' of companies which offers management and financial services to house buyers, sellers and developers and letting services to landlords and tenants within both the residential and commercial sectors.

Over the last four years, I have also developed my own retail nirvana in North Staffordshire, investing in commercial property and developing one of the best beauty destinations in the north of England known as '81 Rose Garden' which I plan to roll out as a brand.

I was born into a working class family with no one to educate me in business but over the years I have developed the skills needed to be a good negotiator, strategic planner, visionary and financier to create an award-winning business and extensive property portfolio. I hope however that I have never lost touch with my roots, respect for others or the humility that is naturally instilled in me.

What were you doing before you got into business?

Back in the 1980s and early 90s, the mines and the pits were the main industry in Staffordshire and all my friends were either working down the pits or in a potbank (pottery factory).

When I left Biddulph Grammar School I was lucky enough to have choices. I was quite a talented musician who could play trumpet, the flat bass and keyboard and was privileged to have been taught by a famous trombonist, Tom Barlow, who has since sadly passed away.

I was passionate about music and particularly the trumpet. I would practise for two to three hours every single day. It got me to the point where I was selected to play in the Staffordshire Jazz and Brass Band. We performed all over the UK, and abroad, including in front of 4,000 people at The Royal Albert Hall including HRH the Queen. I was only 14 years old at the time and this remains one of my proudest memories. Not bad, for a boy born on the wrong side of the tracks!

Why did you get started? What was the key driver?

When I look back I think I was always a little different to my school mates - many just accepted that a life in the pits or down the mines was a foregone conclusion but I wanted more and was prepared to reach for it. I was constantly weighing up the opportunities that a career in music might afford me. I received the highest examination mark in the Midlands and won a scholarship to the Royal College of Music in Manchester, but with a heavy heart I turned it down. Unless you were a singer, or owned the rights to your own music, a career as a musician was not going to support me. The truth is, and it's largely the same today, that as a session musician, however talented, you can have a great life, but you're not going to get wealthy out of it.

Somehow, I ended up plastering. My granddad was a plasterer, I helped him at weekends occasionally, and then when he sadly passed away I worked in a gang. However, the quality of my work was better than anybody else's, it was the perfectionist in me that meant that my work had to be better than everybody else's, I also had to be quicker than anybody else.

I did everything that I could to stand out within my field, to make sure that I got acknowledged. I used to say: "I don't need to talk, let the job do the talking". And my commitment to workmanship did do the talking, it was noticed by the directors of the company I was working for and the property owners themselves and it led to more work.

I didn't drink when I was younger, I didn't go to the pub like most of the lads, for me it was all about work at that stage.

This is how I see it, while you've got your health and strength, you have the energy to do well in your chosen field, so if you start a business young channel that energy and commitment into your business for the first 20-30 years when your mind and body is at its best.

What did friends and family say when you told them about your business plans?

By 1983, I decided that I wanted to be my own boss. My friends said I'd fail, but that gave me even more determination to do well. They couldn't see that being a plasterer could lead anywhere but I was convinced that with my skills and work ethic I had the potential to build a good business.

It's funny, even though I have long since been involved in residential and commercial development, property lettings and related financial services, many people in Staffordshire still see me as a plasterer rather than an entrepreneur. They often say, "how did you manage to do that?" I might have finally garnered a little respect when the late Lawrie Barratt or Sir Lawrence Barratt of Barratt Homes presented me with one of my first NHBC awards. It was one of my proudest moments. The truth is, I founded my business on sheer hard work, always saving and investing back into my business enterprises and as a result, I have been able to amass a substantial portfolio of properties, many of which I paid cash for. It was the capital growth of those properties that turned me into a millionaire at the age of 32.

What was the hardest part of setting up your businesses?

There are numerous challenges when you're trying to build a business.

The first rule for me (which remains true today) was to make sure my workers got paid every week and there were some weeks when I didn't pay myself. I couldn't because I didn't have sufficient money in the business at that particular time. But after a couple of years of trading, the business grew, our margins improved and I had a healthy bank balance. At that point I started to invest in property and that gave me even greater and greater financial resilience.

Even though I was liquid after a few years I had to learn about accounts and managing a growing business. It was important to show my employees how much I valued them; it was much more than ensuring that my site managers paid my day workers on time, I believed, and still do, in sending them all gifts at Christmas - Marks & Spencer hampers were particularly popular. I'd do the same right up to directorship level. I have learned it's important to value people who work hard for you and are loyal to your business.

I guess the next thing is knowing when to take a risk. I believe you can take a calculated risk once you secure your foundation, as I did with my plastering and property businesses, that's your marker to take calculated risks at the right time to generate growth.

Most businesses need a line of credit at some point, but particularly start ups, whether it's a bank, or your own money, without one you're not doing any business. You're likely to see a unique opportunity that's going to pass you by if you don't grab it. And if you're creative and you've got a vision then the risk factor is low, because you've got that solid foundation in place. This is where a lot of people can make mistakes, trying to grow a business too quickly, over trading, and taking too much risk. If it goes wrong, it's horrible and sometimes the business can't recover. I'm a 'middle risk taker', I've always made sure that I've got some resilience somewhere and that a solid foundation is in place as a Plan B in case things don't work out.

Being successful has a whole host of challenges too and being black has added to that. There were loads of barriers that I had to get through to be acknowledged, I had to let the job do the talking. They didn't judge me, they judged the job, but unfortunately some people judge the person first, before they judge the job. I'm proud to have managed to reverse that way of thinking and now I've got a box at Stoke City Football Club I feel like I am on a level playing field! The other company directors there were delighted for me, knowing that I wasn't born with a silver spoon in my mouth. Success brings lots of positive things but it can be a burden if you don't know how to manage it well. I've seen some people change completely, but I will never change from the person that I was all those years ago.

How long was it before you actually started turning a profit?

When I started out in 1983 I used to pay my cheques directly into the bank every week and as a result I got to know my bank manager who I think saw me as a steady go getting young man. He asked me to reconfigure his home and the job that resulted sealed a long and lasting friendship. As a result he offered me the initial borrowings I needed to buy my first property and effectively send me on my way. After an initial disaster with a business partner over a property refurbishment, I bought a number of terraced houses for about £10,000 a piece in Stoke on Trent and created three levels of finish marketing them as bronze, silver and gold packages. I created a show home and visitor centre for these refurbished properties which had never been done with refurbs before. I marketed them from £39,999 and began to make good money from the late eighties and I was on my way.

From there on I was 'cash rich' and bought properties that were dilapidated, the subject of probate or in a fire sale. I came to agreements with the estate agents marketing them that I would allow them to remarket the houses once my team had renovated them and dressed them for sale. It was this way of working that became my business model – canny purchases, quality workmanship and astute marketing. Needless to say, although most of the properties were sold, I have amassed an extensive personal property portfolio that, over the years, has performed better than my pension plan!

Do you read a lot of books? How do you consume your knowledge currently?

I read a lot. I study, I look at the world economy. I look at what's going on in the UK. I look at forecasts, I've lived through three or four recessions, I understand the market well, I know when to buy.

When everything's down it can only go one way. This goes back to the importance of having liquidity again, money always, always makes money and having money when others don't is important.

When it comes to business I say to myself: "What ability do I have to be able to make that happen? Do I have enough knowledge? Can I educate myself enough?" Even now I'm taking it all in. I'm soaking it up like a wet sponge. I look for niche markets and identify opportunities, for example, I've got £10,000 in the bank, so I ask myself: "How can I make that £10,000 into £20,000?"

I like to identify talent myself. Only last week, I noticed that we've got a girl working in our 81 Rose Garden brand (a top Beauty, Nail & Hair Salon based in Newcastle Under Lyme, Stoke on Trent) whose social media is unbelievable. So I went to the manager there and said: "Look, the social media that she's doing is brilliant." I want to get her in and offer her an opportunity to manage our SEO and social media for the group, so that's what she does now, she runs it.

You've got to find strengths in people, haven't you? Everybody's got their strengths and their weaknesses, so if you put everyone's strengths together then you're going to be successful.

How do you manage your time? How do you know what to handle yourself and what to delegate and how do you ensure you get the work life balance right?

I've got construction directors and surveyors, financial advisors and all sorts of other professionals delivering the work so that my time now is spent developing other businesses that I'm involved with. I still work long hours, but I know how to switch off and make time to play golf, go to the races or visit Ronnie Scotts. Because much of what I am involved with is done at a strategic level it still excites and energises me.

What would you do differently if you started again now?

If I did have to do it all again today, then it would be different because the industry and marketplace has changed a lot since the eighties. I think there's a lot more pressure today, the next generation has created that pressure in my opinion. There's a lot more competition too, there weren't many people doing the same thing in my area, around Stoke on Trent when I started out. Technology has played the biggest part in changing things, in an instant you can compare prices for services without even speaking to somebody.

I don't think that there's any perfect solution to navigating the start up and growth of a business. There will always be challenges and roadblocks! I think a strong work ethic, good management, self belief, resilience and vision are critical to success at any point in time. It doesn't matter what you do, as long as you're committed. You should establish good commercial relationships that allow you to buy some credit to get your business going. Business is also a lot to do with how you sell yourself and present yourself to others. And enthusiasm, your enthusiasm will tell somebody whether you really want it or not, or whether you're just going to play at it.

What was your main reason for starting a business?

I had learnt my trade, had a burning ambition to succeed and my work was winning plaudits so it was natural to set up my own business. Some people prefer the security of employment, others like me, don't want to work for anyone else.

Which is your favourite entrepreneur quote? If you don't have one, make one up!

'The biggest risk is not taking any risk. In a world that changes really quickly the only strategy that is guaranteed to fail is not taking risks.'

– Mark Zuckerberg

If you weren't doing what you do now, what job do you think you would be doing?

I'd probably have taken a managerial role. I tend to think that I can lead, I like to learn and educate, so I'd be a leader. I still feel that it's a pity not to have been able to fulfil a career as a musician but I'm sure I made the right choice.

Do you think there is a point in an entrepreneur's life when they think they have "made it?" And if so, what is that point?

Entrepreneurs just love the challenge, it's what drives them. I would say that even when they have achieved huge success there's always another interesting opportunity to become involved with. Others of course become philanthropists and set up foundations for the greater good and I applaud them. What is the point unless we all try to make positive change?

What's the best bit of business advice you have been given, or given others?

The best bit of advice that I was given, and that I like to give to others, is to believe in yourself, to be consistent, and have tenacity. Then take one day at a time to achieve bigger and better things. Somebody said: 'Everybody always wants to take the lift, but it's all about taking the steps'.

I always say, reinvest into your own business to avoid borrowing and take calculated risks when your business is in a stable position, where it is delivering consistently good margins and income. Make sure that you are on the ball every single day, every moment of the day, and more importantly, develop good communication with your managers and staff; endorse them, thank them, remind them that they're doing great things for the business and look after them, and, above all, reward them when it counts. I've taken this to a level where my employees are not only my tradesmen and staff, they're part of the family. That's how I operate, because without them, I wouldn't be here and vice versa.

What was the first thing you treated yourself to in celebration of some early success?

I treated myself to a brand new 911 Porsche, in 1999. I paid £89,000 for that car and I bought it outright. I made the purchase after securing and turning thirteen properties in a liquidation sale.

I heard about the properties and did a drive-by. As I was in a cash position I told the agent that I'd buy them all without actually looking at them, however he insisted that I did as there was enormous interest in them and each viewer was adding more to their value by making higher offers. So I thought on my feet, there were thirteen properties including a pub, by the way, and I thought: "Why would the agent want to deal with thirteen individuals that are going to mess him about?" I said this to him: "Listen, I will give you the asking price for them all, I will complete in seven days, I'll give you the proof of funds and get my lawyers in touch immediately, so you can get the whole deal done with no headache." I won the deal and the Porsche was my reward!

Interestingly, one of the properties was near Alton Towers Theme Park, it was an old Post Office. It stood me at only £20,000. I simply cut the grass and cleaned the windows and put it back on the market selling it for £100,000! It's this that has been one of the mainstays of the growth of my business, finding and executing those sweet deals. Somebody once said: "Don't sit down and wait for the opportunities to come. Stand up and make them happen."

TONY TROWERS

Website: http://www.artrowers.co.uk/

LinkedIn: linkedin.com/in/tony-trowers-85769774

Instagram: @pillarboxgroup @81rosegarden

CHAPTER 3

LISA PALMER

Lisa Palmer has achieved so much, from a very difficult starting place. From struggling academically with dyslexia, being put down by teachers as a child who said that she wouldn't amount to much, to leaving a relationship, all before setting up her matchmaking business.

What's brilliant is that Lisa followed her passion, she always loved introducing people to each other and so turned that into her business and played to her natural strengths. It takes a lot of courage to strike out on your own and start again from nothing, especially when you have a child to look after and part-time jobs to do to afford to put food on the table.

Tell us about your business ventures?

Well, we have a lot happening just now. 2021 is going to be a busy year! I am working on a new TV show with the amazing Marion Farrelly. Marion was responsible for *X Factor* and *Celebrity Big Brother*, so watch this space. I have a new book out on 27 March called *The D word*, "when he's got to go, he's got to go." This book is aimed at women who need to exit a bad relationship.

We also launched our new women's portal called Mogul Love Community on the same day in March. The portal is a great new place for women to meet new friends, get professional help, learn new life skills and hobbies as well as shop!! Coupled with this is the launch of our new women's charity Mogul Freedom. This charity will help women who have fallen on very hard times and just need a lift up, support, help, love and a roof over their head for a short period of time.

We also have Mogul Vision, our TV and video production company, although business has slowed because of Covid.

Mogul Private Office is our property company.

My main business is Mogul Matchmakers, a matchmaking service, that's my passion, that's what I love to do.

I now also write for a couple of papers and online magazines.

Was the Mogul Group your first business?

No, I had an online dating site, which failed. You need so much money to invest to keep plugging away which back in the day I didn't have. Also, I just didn't really like it because I'm more of a people person and being purely online, it just wasn't me. I was always fearful that something could happen on there. If something happened (to someone on a date) it's on me and my company and I would feel absolutely horrendous. I just couldn't control it the way I wanted to so I closed it down.

Prior to that, I had another business with my ex-husband which was an electrical company.

That was successful, but when we first started we didn't have a penny, I had to think outside the box to generate new work. If the council was doing a development or someone was putting on an extension, I would put a handwritten letter through their post box so we could be the first in line before they were even thinking about an electrician and things like that.

One of the problems though was it wasn't really my passion; I love matchmaking and dating!

Have you ever had a "regular" employed job?

I'd worked in a finance office for years with about 200 women doing admin finance, it was lovely, but also horrendous at times.

I'd had a problem from back at school with Dyslexia. We knew what it was but there wasn't really much help and you were kind of put in a corner a lot and made to feel a bit of a dunce.

Just sitting there 9-5 in an office, or 9-3 at school, I couldn't be myself. I'm quite creative and a people person, so being in an office just sitting in the chair I found very difficult. I'm quite full of energy and it was like being shut in a box and not being able to be myself.

How has dyslexia affected you in your current roles?

I'd suffer with things like writing an email, if I wrote one in the early days you literally couldn't read it! Just writing two paragraphs to a client would take me half an hour because I'd have to keep re-reading it. Even if I just sent out ten emails, that could take me a day.

I decided I needed to do more writing which gave me a kick up the backside because I did actually write my first book years ago. Admittedly I tore it up because I thought, yeah, that's crap!

Financially, starting a business is a struggle, you haven't got a lot of money so I started swapping services with other people. I was quite creative so I could do a video for somebody and I'd get someone to do my admin or typing for me. Now, I wrap a good team around me, so whatever I'm not good at, I've got someone in the team who is good at it.

What was the driver for you setting up your own business?

I'm so passionate about matchmaking, I first started doing it when I was 17 and just started putting people together - I love seeing people together and happy. So, one reason was passion. Secondly, I was doing something that not everybody else was already doing. I wanted to be the best so I trained as a relationship coach, a dating coach, a life coach and an image coach and now have other experts who do that for me.

I'm able to then guide my clients on how I can help them on the right path to finding love.

How did you get started?

When I parted from my husband and walked out of my marriage, I had £250, a bag of clothes, a cheese and pickle sandwich and my son. That's all I had. I had no money. I had nothing.

I had to start from scratch, it was a really difficult time for me, I had no home, I had nothing. And I'm very independent, ambitious and driven. I kept thinking I'm not throwing this away, I'm getting my success, I want my own TV show, I want everything.

I borrowed a little bit of money from my Mum and Dad and I bought a mobile home and had to live in that and start all over again. Trying to bring up your son with no money, trying to buy Christmas presents when you can't, is a very difficult time.

Every penny I earned through doing little part-time jobs, I put towards training, which I did so that I could be the best there was. When I had the qualifications, I built the website myself. I didn't know how to do it, I didn't have a clue how to build a website. It took me a couple of months and if I'm honest, I'd build it and then look at it again and think it's crap. Then I had to get the spelling and grammar checked because I couldn't spell. When I was reasonably happy with the website, I had to get going out there and do it myself, getting business, who's a better advocate for my business than myself?

I was going to events, networking, it was hard work, it was long hours, it was tiring but I was trying to support my family.

Was there ever a point when you thought you would have been better off just getting a regular 9-5 job?

When you're trying to support your son and you can't even buy Christmas presents, you do sit there and think, "oh, God, what's the point of living?" I just gave myself a massive kick up the ass and thought right, no more self-pity, you've got to go out there and do it. I had my part-time job and as long as I had enough money to put food on the table, I could grow my business.

I couldn't go on holiday, I couldn't buy the new car. I just put every penny back into the business. I think you have to be very passionate, and you have to be driven. I could see where I was going to be in the next five to ten years and I knew I was going to achieve my goals, I just had to work bloody hard and sacrifice things to get there.

What was the feedback from family and friends when you told them you were setting up a business?

That was really difficult. For me, personally, I asked a lot of family and friends, and everyone thought I was mad. They brushed me off as being stupid and it really hurt. I think you just have to listen to your gut and not listen to other people too much.

You can take in some of their comments, but don't take in their negativity. Some people I was talking to had never run a dating agency or matchmaking agency. They hadn't even run any business, they worked for a company, so they didn't understand. My advice is it's better if you work in a start-up business to find a mentor, maybe in the same industry, for advice and feedback and don't go to someone who can't relate to being an entrepreneur, they don't understand.

Some people will be jealous of your plans or the fact they haven't done it and will just try to put you down.

School made me very driven. One of my teachers said, "you'll end up in McDonald's" and I just thought, "OK, that's fine, I'll prove you wrong."

How long did it take to make your first bit of proper money?

About eight months roughly, it wasn't quick. Once I had built the website I had to get out there. I couldn't afford proper PR so I was literally pounding the streets and going to so many events, sometimes not getting home until 10 or 11 o'clock at night, it was exhausting. I was doing my part-time job during the day, going home and sorting my sons food out and then going out to an event. It really was exhausting but I kept thinking that this is what I want to do, so I've got to do it. You have to make sacrifices.

What was the hardest part of setting up the business?

It was the juggling act. Doing the part-time job, being a mother, setting the business up and finding the drive to do this with everything else going on. I think when you are a parent there is always the feeling of guilt that you haven't spent enough time with your kids, or played with them enough. When you get home from work you are already knackered, but the kids want to play, you also have to find enough energy to keep working on your own business.

It was also managing my friendship circles, a lot of them hadn't run a business, or didn't have their own business, and some are very wealthy. When they all used to go on holiday and my son used to say, "such and such is going away on holiday", well there was no way I could afford it. I was putting every penny back into the business. That was a really hard time because you feel bad as a parent because you can't provide your kids with all the nice things, but I sat down one day and thought back to when I was a child and all I really wanted was food, a roof over my head and love. I think as long as you can give these three elements, and try to make sure they're happy, then I think you are doing a good enough job.

How many times did you question yourself on whether you have done the right thing in setting up the business and making the sacrifices you had to make?

At least once a week I would question myself. Some weeks it was most days if I was having problems landing a client, for example. It was often when I was having to go to more and more events to try and get business, but money was running low.

I think it is really important to try and stay as healthy as possible. I believe in the mantra of 'healthy body, healthy mind'. If you can't afford to go to the gym, just going out for a walk is good for you and trying to eat healthily because you need as much energy as you can to start and run a business.

As the business began to grow, when did you know it was the right time to take on a new member of staff?

You need to make sure you are earning enough money to be able to do it and make sure that the money you spend on someone is going to help you make more money. I needed to make sure I had enough money coming in to pay the bills and that I wasn't just relying on one client coming in to make sure I could pay for things including someone else's salary.

To grow a business, you need to take risks, but at the same time you do need to be sensible and make sure they are only calculated risks. Having someone with the right drive and ambition is really important and they should want to provide the same level of service to your clients as you do. I've also learned how important it is to look after your staff in order to get the best out of them, but it is a fine line between being their friend and still being their boss.

What has been your biggest mistake in business so far?

I think it was when I started out, expecting that I was going to be rich straight away. I think really to start a business and to grow it to somewhere where you want it to be you're looking at least five years. You obviously will have ups and downs in this period but being your own boss can be amazing and you can really see where you can go and plan how to get there. The first few years are really difficult and you will make mistakes but you get past them and learn from them.

Which parts of the business did you outsource when you started and have you brought them back in-house?

As I said, I used to swap things I couldn't do with people who could do them and I would help them in ways that I could. Probably the first thing I outsourced was my admin as my dyslexia meant I struggled with it. I could deal with the accounts, I could deal with clients, but it was the writing and admin I couldn't do. I now surround myself with brilliant staff who can do this for me.

How did you know when you could pay yourself a wage and still keep investing in the business?

It took a good few years at least because I was paying everyone else and my bills first. I was running on fresh air and only really paying myself my expenses. Once I saw the account balance rising, I knew I could pay myself something although I still only paid myself what I needed and still kept putting more back into the business.

I have always been raised not to waste money and my family have run businesses so I know you have to look after the pennies! I now do spend money but I invest in properties through another business I own called Mogul Private Office.

Has starting and running a business overall been easier or harder than you thought it would have been?

Harder! I should have realised it really as I saw my family running businesses, but I always had my vision board which had things like having my own TV show written on it which helped keep me focused.

I also have my mantras: 'Right thoughts, right words, right actions'. I have now achieved most of my vision board including a big house so the hard work has paid off! I am also working on my own TV show. Think big and be positive.

If you were to start it all again today, what if anything would you do differently?

I don't think I would do anything differently apart from not asking people who hadn't got or run their own business for their opinion on what I was doing. If I got 100 positive bits of feedback my mind would go to the one negative bit I got and that isn't helpful.

How do you manage your time?

It's bloody hard! Having a good team around you helps and so does learning how to delegate. I was also super-organised, where I used to cook meals on a Sunday and freeze them so I always ate in the week and doing things like this helped me stay focused.

What are the three most important qualities an entrepreneur should have?

Drive. Thick skin to deal with the knockbacks and finally, as before, healthy mind and body - really important!

What is the most important lesson you have learned in business?

Get up, put your positive face on and get back out there. Every day is a new day, as one door closes another one opens. It's all about the positive mental attitude.

"Your life is only good as your psyche" - Lisa Palmer

What was the main reason for starting a business?

Avoiding working for someone else was a big thing for me, but also being put down at school by teachers who said I wouldn't ever do anything with my life gave me the drive I needed to do my own thing. And of course, financial freedom!

What do the next five years look like?

I have another book coming out. I would love to be the next Oprah Winfrey, maybe in the next ten years!

What is your favourite entrepreneurial quote?

I don't know if it's an entrepreneurial quote or not, but I do believe things can change in a minute, an hour or a day. Don't be disheartened if something doesn't go your way, another opportunity could be just round the corner.

If you weren't an entrepreneur what would you be doing?

I'd be depressed! I couldn't do the whole 9-5, but if I did it would be something with animals, maybe working in an animal home.

Is there a point when you think you will have made it?

No. I could sell my business but I don't want to. My business is my baby, I may take more of a back seat but I'd always be part of it.

What was the first thing you treated yourself to and what is the most extravagant thing you have bought?

A holiday! I did absolutely nothing on it, just laid by the pool! I was exhausted, I needed to recharge my batteries. The most extravagant physical purchase was probably my Range Rover. It's important to treat yourself!

LISA PALMER

www.mogullove.com

www.mogulmatchmakers.co.uk

Instagram: @mogullovecommunity @lisapalmerofficial

CHAPTER 4

MARINOS ALEXANDROU

Marinos Alexandrou is the director and co-founder of International Andrology, which is based in London and manages health centres in Europe and the Middle East. It is a world leading organisation of top physicians and surgeons who have played major roles in the development and improvement of modern surgical techniques in the field of men's sexual and reproductive health. https://london-andrology.co.uk/. Marinos is also the co-founder and director of Adam Health https://talktoadam.com and is on a mission to close the gender health gap encouraging men to seek help from their doctors when they need it.

Marinos is also an expert in hospitality and has owned and been involved in several pub and hospitality venues like the Brass Monkey pub in Victoria, http://brassmonkeylondon.co.uk/ and the Camden Grocer https://www.thecamdengrocer.com/.

He is also a co-founder of the award-winning artisan beer 56 Isles in the Greek Islands https://56islesbeer.gr/microbrewery/

In addition to his other directorships within the healthcare, leisure and f&b sectors in London, Marinos has a background in advising businesses on Mergers & Acquisitions and Fundraising and Investments. Marinos was born in Cyprus and has an MSc in finance from Cass Business School at the University of London.

You're a serial entrepreneur, can you tell us about yourself and your businesses?

I was born and spent my early years in Cyprus. After a short time in the army, I came to the UK to study and started working in finance before venturing out into my own business. From a very early age I was interested in business and had projects on the go. I knew I wanted to start my own business, so I began looking at opportunities when I was working in finance and ended up co-founder of International Andrology - a medical business which focuses on men's health across Europe and the Middle East. Since then I have co-founded an online Med-Tech business called Adam Health developing a telemedicine platform. These are the main focus of my business activity although I have a passion for the hospitality sector too and I am also involved in London pubs and f&b businesses, a deli turned online grocery store (due to Covid-19) and also a micro-brewery in one of the Greek Islands.

What were you doing before you set up the businesses?

Going back to my student days, I always aspired to be a "businessman". My father was in business, my grandmother was in business and both ran family businesses. I was inspired by the fact that you could build something from an idea and become financially independent.

I looked at opportunities that I could be involved in. I was organising trips away or planning activities and trying to make money from them. I was managing a pub-like place from a very early age, a meeting place which I treated like a business venture. I started importing things from Europe and selling them.

I tried to use platforms for selling things like clothes, as my father was in the clothing business and then looked into selling cars. I would travel over to Germany, buy cars and then bring them down to Greece. I was doing whatever would get me interested and excited, I wanted to feel the adrenaline and the excitement of being successful within my own means and gaining financial independence. As a result of this, I had my own money from a young age, and I remember my mother being really confused with how I always had money which was more than my allowance. My parents recognised that I was into business but my mother was a little bit worried that I may have ended up doing something I shouldn't be doing! Selling the cars was the wildest venture I had back then as I was just a kid. I was buying cars from Germany and didn't speak a word of German, so ended up taking a friend with me there who spoke a little of the language which made it more interesting.

Why did you get started in business?

Financial independence was a motivator when I was younger. There were things I wanted like a nice car. I remember I really wanted a BMW when I was about 18 or 19, but couldn't ask my parents for it, so I had to earn my own money.

However, I can't say I have ever been massively driven in business by the financial side. Being financially independent or financially successful comes with being successful in business. That was the driver for me - but, it is a really long time before you get there. There are times of uncertainty, times when you have put all of your money into the venture with the result that you are only just managing.

The "Why" for me is that I was always fascinated by the personalities of entrepreneurs, their energy, their conviction, their vision and their success in life. From a young age I knew I wanted to be like these people, people who had their own businesses, who had an idea and they put it to work.

How did you get started in business?

Starting out, when I was working in finance, I was looking into what was hot, what interested me or what looked like a good opportunity at that moment in time. I started out with pubs because there was a time when they were cheap to acquire and I was interested in buying a pub that wasn't doing well, turning it around and either selling it or maybe putting it in a portfolio. That's actually how I started in business in the UK and that led me to understanding the financial engineering behind business and how to put together a structure for managing things. I didn't necessarily have the time to do everything because I was still working full-time, but this acted as a precursor to helping me put together a structured business plan and then posing the question: 'this is my creation, this is how I expand it, this is how I approach clientele, this is how I source, procure, hire and fire'. It was a massive learning curve.

My curiosity, my drive and my energy were communicated to people like my family and friends. I was always coming up with ideas and saying: "Wow, this is interesting", or I would find out something from someone and be inquisitive about how it works.

I was fortunate enough to have friends who I could talk to and partner with for my different ideas. As part of the diversified interests in my portfolio I partnered up with different people where we could put together our ideas and make something out of them and that is how I was able to manage things in different industries. Then came the ideas with the clinics and the medical practices which have become my most successful and ground-breaking ventures. The pubs and other interests are successful, but they operate on a smaller scale. With the clinics and the medical and management teams we put together for them, it quickly became clear that they could become a big business and scale out internationally.

What did friends and family say when you told them you were setting up in business?

I'm a person of conviction, if I have conviction about something and I believe in an idea, whether that is my idea or someone else's, and I shape a view on something, I will work to make something happen. I'm not saying you can't change your mind, or can't be proven wrong, in business, as in life, it is so dynamic and you always have options, but when I have a conviction about something, especially in business, I will do what I think I ought to be doing. So in that sense, I didn't really come across too much negativity but maybe that's because my circle of friends and family know I am very positive and embrace my excitement about things.

There were some people who were telling me to make sure I was being careful, and I listened to those views, but I wouldn't ever let that hold me back if I believed that it was something I should be doing. I was fortunate that my friends understood my excitement for business; in fact some said that I had created an aura around me that meant that people came to me with their ideas and together we were able to do things. This has led me into multiple ventures with friends, associates and business partners. Over the years I have had much more positive feedback from family and friends than the pessimistic feedback.

What were the first priorities you had when setting up the business?

When we started up the clinics I already had a couple of ventures on the side so my plate was already quite full. We talked about the idea of the clinics with my business partner who was already a very good friend of mine and we said let's try it out, let's test it in the UK and see what happens.

The first 'soft' priority we had was to put together the website and we already had ideas on how to market it and how to attract interest from our target group. The really difficult first priority was finding the right physical space and trying to set up a business within the many sub-frameworks (of healthcare). It's not easy as a non-medical person to put together a medical business in the private sector. Finding regulated space in healthcare is very difficult alone. There are a lot of boxes that you need to tick and it's a different evolution from 'just' being a doctor and slowly putting together a practice. You have to be au fait with all of the regulations and compliance to demonstrate to people that you can be trusted to deliver high quality care and services.

That was one of our biggest challenges, finding the right clinical space. We started with a small practice in central London but then we had to find the right doctors who trusted us with delivering the service.

Away from setting up the clinical business, looking back at the pub ventures you couldn't be considered as a pub landlord or proprietor if you didn't have experience, but you couldn't get experience if you didn't have a pub! How I got round this was I bought a cheap lease of a pub just to get that on my CV so I would be considered by the bigger breweries when I put in an application to acquire a larger site.

Was there any moment when you thought you may have made a mistake and that you should have just stayed in the finance world as an employee?

No. I never looked back and thought I should have stayed here, or done this, or done that instead. There were times of frustration, but I never doubted that I had done the right thing. There were times when people would tell me about someone who I used to work with who was now earning a lot of money, but as an entrepreneur there's a journey in life and sometimes success comes either very early or a bit later on, you have ups and downs, but there was never a time when I felt I should have stayed working in finance or not got involved in my various business ventures.

How long did it take you to earn your first bit of money as an entrepreneur?

It's hard to quantify that as I always looked at my profit as an opportunity cost for a new business, so I was always rolling over that money into developing the business further or new ventures. I've always viewed what money I have as potential capital investment for my next venture. For example, when we put together the brewery in Greece (56islesbeer. gr), everyone thought I was mad because it was off the back of one of the biggest financial crises in European history! But I had my reasons and I had a strong conviction that it would work.

In the first year of setting up business, what was the hardest decision you had to make?

There are always hard decisions to make, such as foregoing nice things or going out a lot because you don't want to spend that money, but one of the hardest was how to manage my time along with the other things I was doing and in the very early days, whether I should completely quit my day job and just focus on my business. There was a sequence of hard decisions that I had to make about when to stop doing one thing and start on another. In some ways there was a feeling of guilt about neglecting one area or letting something go.

When did you know that it was the right time to take on your first member of staff?

In any of my businesses it is 'when the penny drops' and I realise that I don't have time to be doing all of these things, even with the help of my business partners. At that point we weigh up the opportunity versus the cost. And in any start-up, it's not like you have a lot of money! It's when I take a step back and see that this thing is growing, the proof of concept is there and it's time to take on another pair of steady hands. It's important to look at a number of candidates, success lies in finding the kind of people that you can work closely with and create great things with. I want to make sure that people can see the opportunity for a career and that they have a desire to stay with you for the long run. And there's also a responsibility to them if I make them an offer and say that they can forgo their job somewhere else, I need to sell my vision to them and make them comfortable that they have a future with my business.

Were there any parts of your businesses that you chose to outsource, to maximise your time and profits?

If it's a core function of the business then I'm a big believer in doing things in-house, because at the end of the day you have to get those fundamentals exactly right to deliver the best product or service - whether that's to clinic patients or customers coming into a pub for a meal or buying a beer. Customers need to be happy and content to be paying you for that service or that offering. When it comes to material parts of the business, it of course makes sense to be sensible about your suppliers, for example we are not going to be able to make the glass bottles to put our beer in, or the consumables for the clinic. Once businesses start growing then we begin to outsource things, like for example marketing, to agencies that are the experts in that field.

In the early days, how did you know how much money to pay yourself out of the businesses, or did you keep reinvesting?

I kept reinvesting and growing the business in the hope that it did sufficiently well to determine my remuneration based on success. I base what I pay myself on how much I need to invest into the business at that time. And it's funny because a lot of people have this misconception that because you have a few businesses you must have millions in the bank and enjoy a very comfortable life - in my case, the reality is that whatever I make, I put it back in!

Was starting a business harder or easier than you thought it would be?

Now that's a very interesting question! I didn't actually have a preconception of how hard it would be. There are certainly still times when I think: "Oh man, this is so hard!" in situations that are extremely difficult. If I'm honest I think that the desire to start to develop something always made things feel a little easier. Sometimes I look back and think: "How did I do that?"

If you take a step back, look at everything you've achieved, mistakes you've made and could take a magic step back and start all over again, would you do anything differently?

With hindsight, there are certainly some small things that I might have done differently, but my main answer to that would be 'no'. At the end of the day, being in business and making things happen is a constant learning curve, you are going to make mistakes but that is part of the journey.

Now that you are an established businessman, do you have a process or planned approach for how to best manage your time?

I'm not sure when one becomes an "established businessman" but I'm ashamed to say that I still don't have that process in place! There are always long days and lots of things to juggle, but actually one of the things that came out of the Coronavirus pandemic is that it's made me take a different view of some stuff in my life. I've made a conscious decision to devote more time to my personal commitments and block portions of time out for that, otherwise my days and weeks always end up being longer than I thought.

In your opinion, what are the three most important qualities that an entrepreneur should have?

You have to be happy in what you are doing.

You have to be creative - business is all about creating opportunities and experiences as well as products and services.

You have to have or develop conviction. Almost on a daily basis you will come to crossroads where you need to make decisions, sometimes difficult ones, so you need to have that instinct to be able to make the right choices.

What does the next five years look like for you?

I took a long-term view, even from a very young age. I always looked ahead and knew that I wanted to be in business. Over the next five years, ideally, I would like to still be operating in the healthcare business that I am focusing on now and steadily growing it. I have visions for where I would like to be, and not just financial and growth ones either, I have visions for society as well, in terms of what I could contribute. I want to make sure that I am still on the same path, and if I've reached those goals in five years then good, and if I've achieved some of them and continued to learn on the journey then that's still fine.

Do you have a favourite inspirational quote?

It's not really a quote, but I really do think that an entrepreneur should:

'Be happy and be creative'.

If you hadn't started your own businesses, what do you think you would be doing now instead?

I possibly would have just stayed working in finance, but I think if I had my time again, or a parallel life, then I'd want to have been an artist, maybe a musician. In fact, two years ago I bought a piano, but never got round to starting lessons, but in line with my goal for next year to make time for personal development, I have now started piano lessons.

Do you think that there is ever a point in an entrepreneur's life when they think that they've 'made it'?

No, I don't think there is. I personally have never, ever felt that there is a stopping point ahead, where I will stop exploring interesting opportunities.

What was the first thing that you treated yourself to when you

In the early days I bought the BMW that I really wanted, but I sold it after a few months to make some money on it! It was the desire to have that car that led me to creating a business out of it when I was still a student. I also bought a really nice watch at one point, which, like the car, I had coveted. As it turned out, that watch has risen in value over the years and turned out to be a good investment, which is great!

MARINOS ALEXANDROU

London Andrology: https://london-andrology.co.uk
Adam Health: https://talktoadam.com
Brass Monkey pub: http://brassmonkeylondon.co.uk
The Camden Grocer: https://www.thecamdengrocer.com
56 Isles Brewery: https://56islesbeer.gr/microbrewery

CHAPTER 5

TYRONE MINGS

We were so honoured that Aston Villa and England defender Tyrone Mings agreed to talk to us and feature in our first book. Without a doubt Tyrone is one of the nicest, most humble guys that we've spoken with, and he's known for his great work off the pitch as well as on it. He is actually a qualified mortgage broker, and tells us here about his passion project side hustle which is an interior design business. It is fascinating to read about how someone who has achieved many a schoolboy's dream has made sure that he doesn't take things for granted and has a solid 'Plan B' too.

Give us an introduction to your 9-5 day job and also your side hustle.

My day job is being a professional footballer. It is multifaceted as I have a club career with Aston Villa and also an international career playing for England. The two run parallel with each other and also overlap at various times. The club career is very much Monday-Friday with games on the weekend and probably the bulk of my identity is as a footballer in the premier league.

The international side is a whole new world in terms of exposure, publicity and criticism. If you play for England everyone in England has an opinion on it. If you play for Aston Villa, people who support Aston Villa will critique or praise your performance and that is something that takes a lot of getting used to.

My side hustle is an interior design company I set up when I was playing for Bournemouth. I met my business partner down in Bournemouth when she had just finished university so the timing worked really well which meant that the business grew out of Bournemouth and by meeting great people the business was able to flourish down there. It has now grown from being mainly a residential interior design company to more of a commercial interior design company doing lots of restaurants, nightclubs, offices and retail spaces and it has grown organically over the last five years.

I am very fortunate that I am able to be passionate about the two things I am doing both in my day job and my side hustle.

You have a well-known passion for property, was it this passion that made an interior design company an obvious choice as a side line?

I have a property background which gave me a good footing into the industry. A lot of people's side hustle business ideas are born out of their passion and things they are interested in or where they can see a gap in the market. I guess mine was a bit of both, I'd not long come out of being a mortgage advisor when I crossed paths with my business partner and I'd just got into the premier league and felt I was ready for my first business venture and thought I was at I point where I could explore other things away from football. This was back in 2015 and long-term I was thinking property development might be a good way for me to diversify my investments and make some money and secure my family's future. I knew about buying and selling properties but didn't necessarily know about flipping and running a project from start to finish. I came into the business with an element of wanting to learn the industry and have been fortunate enough to be surrounded by great people who have not only taught me as we have been going along but also helped the company develop and have given us opportunities that perhaps wouldn't have been afforded to us without the energy, and naivety if I'm honest, that comes with being new business owners.

How important do you think it is to be passionate about the industry that your side hustle is in?

Hugely important. It's the passion that drives you through the tough times. There is no route to success, whatever success looks like to you, that will come easy. You go through a lot of crap and setbacks and when you are in those periods and questioning yourself, passion is the most authentic thing that keeps you going. If you can maintain the passion for as long as possible it will keep you in good stead.

How did you know that your business partner would be a good person to start a business with?

I didn't know at the start. I think it's impossible to get trust straight away. We had gone to school together, but weren't in the same friendship groups, we knew of each other but weren't connected yet. We knew a lot of the same people so that helped bring a small element of trust as there would have been too many people involved if we had screwed each other over. It was only after a conversation with her and tapping into her passion for interior design that I knew she would be successful with me or with someone else.

It was a leap of faith but having had more and more conversations around the opportunity and what we wanted the company to stand for we knew we could make it work. We had the chat about me putting money in, but obviously with a football career I couldn't put the man hours in like she could. Having her respect that made me reciprocate that respect to her and that built trust. Trust is hard to come by and when you find it in people, it's invaluable.

Looking back at it now, we had no reason not to trust each other. She knew I was in a world from where I understood property and I could see the passion that she had.

Would you have considered a side hustle just by yourself without a business partner?

I have a few different side hustles going on and I've never wanted to venture into it alone. That is probably because my football career takes up so much time in my head. Monday to Wednesday is spent reflecting on the previous game, Thursday, Friday and Saturday is spent on the next game so that leaves very little room in my head to think about a sole project and how to make it successful. I don't really have the energy to do it all so I have always invested in good people to have around me to help. It's important to have a solid group of people around me who can tap into my strengths at the right time, but my strengths aren't fundamental to the success of the business. KTM would have been successful even if I wasn't there, but I wouldn't have made it a success without the other people involved in it.

In the things that have gone well in my life, like football, I have a whole team of people around me including chefs, masseurs, psychologists, etc, and these are people who I can tap into at different times of the week and use them for different things.

What was the driver for setting up a side hustle?

Probably a mixture of three things. The first was to make me a better-rounded human. In football you are in a bit of a bubble, you are immersed into a world that isn't really reality, for example most people have to ring their GP and wait to see them, I can ring the club doctor at midnight and be having a scan the next morning. The business really allowed me to create an identity when things in football weren't going well. I set KTM up in the same month I got injured and it allowed me to create a new identity as a business person. It also gave me a chance to be more mentally stable, if I had ploughed all of my focus into just football and then it's taken away from me then naturally that came with some unstable months mentally. KTM really helped me in those few months.

Secondly, it gave me an opportunity to learn. I set KTM up to help me learn about the industry which may sound a little strange, why wouldn't I just try and learn from speaking to other people? But I learn best by doing things. I have set up businesses in multiple industries to learn about multiple things. I could read books, and I love reading, but it wouldn't show me personally what the industry is like.

Lastly it was to create a business. I wanted to create a business to prove to myself that I could do it and make a long-term business. It is probably different from many people who set up a business as I didn't do it for the money, I haven't taken a penny out of KTM in the five years we have had it. When Covid-19 hit, we were quite fortunate that we didn't need to furlough anyone as we had grown the business organically, we had never over stretched ourselves above our means which worked for us.

Was it a simple decision that you were going to set up KTM as a side hustle?

It was really simple. I had a couple of meetings with my business partner, sat in the foyer area of the university, and we spoke about how it had to be something she was passionate about as she would be running the majority of the company's affairs. I was based in Bournemouth at the time so that made things quite simple. Even the name of the company came to me whilst I was sitting on the toilet!

We didn't need it all to be perfect before we started. It was a case of we had the name, we can knock a website together quite quickly and after that it was just a case of networking the shit out of it, which is exactly what we did. It really was an easy decision.

What would be your advice to someone looking at starting up a side hustle? And what would you advise them against?

I think one thing you should do is have a clear reason for starting the side hustle. For me, I know my business ventures will never supersede what I am doing with football so I am comfortable with it always being a side hustle. That may change when I stop playing though. This really helped when dealing with the problems as they can then be dealt with with an element of perspective. OK, they are problems, and business problems, but it wasn't like I was relying on the business or money from the business to put food on the table or a roof over my head.

Many people will start a side hustle with the intention of building it up to take over their normal 9-5 and if that is why you start then that may come with some problems and pressure but this is where you need to keep your end goal in mind.

What I would say to avoid is procrastination. I actually have a tattoo on my chest which reads "assassination of procrastination". I am actually awful at it, but every time I look in the mirror it gives me a kick. It's the killer of dreams, belief and momentum. MVP or minimal viable product is about getting something out there which doesn't need to be perfect. You may not think it is perfect but someone who is seeing it for the first time won't know what it should be looking like, or what version two will look like, so get a plan together and run with it. Don't procrastinate. Things change constantly and that is part of being successful in business and really anything, the ability to adapt to change. We are living in a world right now where everybody has been forced to change with Covid-19 and the companies who will come out stronger and ready to run again when we come out of this pandemic will be the ones who have been able to adapt to change. You don't need things to be perfect to start, but you do need to start.

Your 'day job' is totally different to your side hustle, have there been any transferable skills from one to the other?

Yes, absolutely. My people skills and the ability to empathise emotionally and understand different people has been learnt in football, dealing with egos, attitudes, beliefs, etc. In business this has helped me as we have started working with more and more people and understanding that people are different and how to deal with different people based on their status, journey in the industry, etc. Whilst we try to treat everyone the same, this can be dangerous. Sometimes we need to put an arm around people when they need it and others we don't. I was involved in the Black Lives Matter campaign this year which teaches us about equality and equity. Equality means you should treat everyone exactly the same whereas equity says that you treat people, or give people slightly more based on their starting position or what they need at that certain point. Being in the football world has opened my eyes to so many different types of people and having a voice in the changing room has helped me see that sometimes you need to put an arm around people, and other times on the pitch for example I may need to shout at them to give them a kick up the ass as that will get the best out of them.

How do you keep the two worlds separate - ensuring that a bad result on a Saturday does not impact a client meeting on a Monday?

It's pretty easy really. Compartmentalising is important in a side hustle. If you're going to do a side hustle, you need to be pretty fucking good at separating the two jobs you have. It's a danger that you let one role affect the other. My life is multifaceted, whether running the football academy, or setting up the new one in Barbados, or the app, or the design company or being an elite athlete, all of which I have chosen to do. If I choose to do something and my name is attached to it there comes a certain level of pride with it, but I still need to be able to park one thing and put on another hat.

What was the hardest thing about setting up the side hustle?

Probably managing my time. Geographically I was in Bournemouth so it was relatively ok but I was still having to rush from one thing to another. I was doing a lot of networking, maybe too much, but it's hard to say how much of that attributed to the success of the company, so it was probably worth it. It's a very fine balance between getting involved, and not getting too involved. When I was injured it probably felt like I had more time as I wasn't playing on a Saturday but in reality I had less time because I spent time worrying about my injury and I was in London, Philadelphia and Qatar for rehab.

What, if any, analysis of the interior design market did you do before starting up?

My business partner had a good knowledge of interior design, and what we were actually going to be doing, but neither of us had life experience because of our ages. At that point I was 22 and had been through pretty much everything negative you can think of. I had also worked in the real world, in pubs, retail, offices and building sites so I had some knowledge of working.

In terms of analysis of the market, there's a fine line between procrastination and doing nothing, and doing too much. You can never do enough that it will really prepare you for your business problem, we learned a lot of things on the job, and we are still learning. If I'm being brutally honest, we used what experience and knowledge we had and just ran with it.

What is the first thing people should be doing when they have an idea for a side hustle?

The first thing I did was speak to as many people as I could who had walked a similar path to what we were going to be doing. We have just taken on a property development project in Bournemouth so I asked a property developer in Birmingham about it. This works as it doesn't conflict with what he is doing as he's doing much bigger things but I do get honest advice from him. I would absolutely speak to three or four different people who don't have a vested or conflicted interest in what you are doing, perhaps even in different industries as there are lessons you can learn. People can't tell you what to do, you need to take in what is useful and use it to create your own roadmap.

Do you think you will always have multiple side hustles even after football?

I think I will always have side hustles. I think not only does it give me more layers as a person, but I also get such different feelings from business than football. Placing all your eggs in one basket can be dangerous, for example to your mental health, if that all goes wrong. I think having a business contributes a lot to me being a better person and a better-rounded individual.

Also, I don't think a side hustle always needs to be a business that makes money. For example, I am learning to play the piano, something that gives me an escape from what I am known for.

What has been the best and worst day of your side hustle so far?

Not so much a worst day, more of a worst period, was probably when we started out and we were getting turned down a lot as people thought we didn't know what we were doing. To them we were a couple of 22 year old kids running around trying to create people's workplaces or homes. When they asked for our portfolio not only did we not have one, we also didn't have the experience to show we could do the job. This period was hard as we had to overcome this quickly. We weren't just doing this for fun, we needed to prove that our passion and energy would overcome any problems.

The best day was probably when we did our first nightclub. It was a large project with great marketing around it. It was also one of the first jobs we did where not only did we do the design, we were also doing the project management as well. Normally the interior design is a small part of the overall project so we would submit our designs but wouldn't have any control over the final quality, so for this we had our own Project Manager which brought about its own challenges, but ultimately gave us much more control.

What does the next five years look like for KTM?

Continual growth and learning. I would be the proudest of KTM if I can sit here in five years and can say we are still learning and growing and making wise decisions - that would represent success to me.

I will also be proud if we continue to grow organically rather than trying to overstretch ourselves which can often ruin a business if we had no other work because everyone was tied up in one big project, for example. It will be a successful five years if we can keep the reins on and not try to run before we can walk.

What is the best bit of business advice you have been given?

It's not so much spoken advice, more a learning that you don't always have to have the answers. I always try to speak to people who are successful in their own business but they don't always have the answer, so they can't give me the answer. You are in control of your business, you can find examples and say that if Covid-19 didn't happen you would have been successful, but if you didn't change in this time and adapt that's not Covid's fault, it's yours. When you can accept responsibility for everything in your life and business it can be really empowering.

If you were to start over again, what would you do differently this time around?

I don't think there is anything I could have or would have done differently. I wouldn't change anything because I've learnt what I've learnt, I've met who I've met and I know what I know and all that has accumulated into me being happy and empowered. I don't think you get those things without going through the hard times.

TYRONE MINGS

Instagram: @tyronemings @tyronemingsacademy
@ktmdesignltd

Twitter: @OfficialTM_3

Websites: www.ktmdesign.co.uk /
https://tyronemingsacademy.com

CHAPTER 6

LESLEY REYNOLDS

Lesley Reynolds' story is a lovely example of having an early dream and keeping laser-focused on it, knowing that you will achieve it eventually. Lesley always wanted to be involved in beauty, skincare and cosmetic work and even knew which beautiful building on Harley Street, London, that she wanted to work in! She needed a job after her divorce and decided to take a beauty course to learn the industry, set up a small salon and her drive and passion has grown the business from there. It really is never too late to start your own business, it doesn't matter what age you are or if you have zero knowledge or experience, 'you don't need to be great to start, but you do need to start to be great.'

Can you tell us a little about your business ventures?

I am the co-founder of Harley Street Skin Clinic which is based in a beautiful building at number 48 Harley Street. The clinic offers the latest treatments and procedures in cosmetic surgery, beauty and skin care. We also undertake regenerative work with stem cells and other cellular treatments and offer revolutionary wound healing treatments.

Over the years, we have built a clientele of over 44,000 patients and had our own television series on Sky back in 2013. However, I am most proud of my team of doctors and therapists who have garnered numerous awards for the clinic.

We also have our own skin care collections. Having worked in the beauty and cosmeceuticals industry, I know a lot about skin care and have developed the Harley Street Skincare collection. My intent was to develop products that were more affordable than I could buy them but to sell them for a higher price. Our various skin care collections are sold in the clinic and online and are really popular. I also help other people develop their own product ranges.

Somehow I have earned the epithet, 'The Queen of Harley Street' for my work. I have written a couple of books and write a weekly column for Best, OK and the Daily Express. However, the clinic takes up most of my time. I am the person who the buck stops with, so if there is a problem with anything it will land on my desk!

I am also co-founder with my husband of the charity Back on Track which rehabilitates injured servicemen. This involves organising fundraising activities and staging events as well as providing ongoing support to our servicemen who need treatment for their physical injuries, therapy for their mental health and financial support.

What were you doing before you set up Harley Street Clinic?

I was actually already working in Harley Street but not at the same place we are now. I had a little practice at the top of Harley Street where I met my husband who owns Harley Street Clinic with me now. I thought that he was a really good doctor and so he began working with me at my clinic and within six months he was full time. I remember walking up and down Harley Street at the time and looking at this really pretty house and imagining it as a clinic. One day I noticed it was empty so I spoke to the people who own the buildings along here about it. The rest is history. We've been here for 11 years!

How do you balance working with your husband and stopping issues in the personal world coming into your professional world?

My husband is Head of Medicine and I run the business so we operate in different parts of the business on a daily basis. However, it is really hard sometimes to separate the work from the personal. If we argue, it is generally about work; we try really hard not to let any issues impact the business or the staff and keep the atmosphere buzzy and the staff upbeat. Quite simply, we have to put any disagreements on hold until we get home. It is lovely though working in the same business as my husband as we can share coffee and lunch during the day and we come and go together.

The harder part is balancing life with the children and grandchildren. I feel like I am married to the job; my kids often ask if I can look after the grandchildren at the weekend, or in the evening, but frequently I have to turn them down which can be difficult for all of us.

Why did you get started?

I got divorced and was still living in the family home, but I didn't have an income. I picked up the phone one day and it had been cut off. I was so young and naive that I didn't realise that's what happened if you didn't pay the bill! I quickly realised that I needed an income and the only person who could do that was me. I took a beauty course as it was the time when lots of people were getting into the industry. It was just before collagen and Botox became popular but I already knew of these new treatments. I opened a tiny beauty salon and grew it from there. I love learning and so when I saw a course for American-based Cosmeceuticals (cosmetic products with bioactive ingredients purported to have medical benefits) I went to the USA to improve my knowledge. When I was there I learned about collagen injections so when I returned I found someone who could do them in my little clinic. It was identifying that new trend that helped me to develop the business.

What did friends and family say
when you first told them?

I didn't really tell them to be honest, I just got on and did it. I told them when I had it all set up and they were supportive then. I think you will always get people who are a bit jealous or detract from your endeavour especially when they see you are doing well. Happily most people close to me have been supportive, but I don't really ask them for their support, or opinions. Actually, if someone had come up to me and told me they didn't think it was a good idea to open a clinic, that would have simply driven me to do it even more. Today, we employ one of my old school friends and some of our family.

What were the first priorities you
had when you started up?

My first one was finding the right premises. I had a clear vision of where I wanted to be. I wanted to be "high end" as I was taught that rich people are always going to have money regardless of what happens, but I didn't want to make the business exclusively for rich people. I wanted it to be available to everyone so now we do treatments across the board ranging from £80 to £60,000 - £70,000 each. Our 'bread and butter' is the people who come in and spend £300 on Botox regularly, not the people who spend the big money a couple of times a year. The average spend is probably about £1,000. We offer finance to help people who want treatment but can't afford it.

What was the hardest part about
getting the business set up?

The lack of funds was the hardest part. My husband and I had both come out of marriages so we didn't have a lot in the early days.

I remember one particular day at the start, my husband and I had to take the room we were working from for a second day in the week as we had more clients booked in than normal. We had decided to go out to dinner that night but only had £60 between us for the meal, thankfully when we got the bill, it came to £59.80! I remember thinking to myself we could have made more money if we had just gone to McDonald's!

We got over the lack of funds by working longer and longer hours. The more money that came in meant we could buy more stock or more equipment. We bought everything outright and never looked at entering into a hire purchase agreement. We had to keep generating an income and this meant working seven days a week for several years.

The challenge then became not a lack of customers, it was a lack of time to fit them all in. Our treatment is instantaneous and we receive payment for it straight away.

Was there ever a moment when you thought you would be better just getting a regular 9-5 job?

No, I never felt like that, it always felt like we were doing the right thing. We were always looking to grow and expand.

What was the hardest decision you had to make when starting the business up?

Really it was whether or not we should rent more rooms to do the treatments in. Although it was good that the money was coming in when we did the treatments, we needed to have more than one person in at a time so we took on another doctor relatively quickly for whom we needed the extra room. We then had to look at whether or not we could afford the rent. However, as I'm a positive person who relies on gut instinct and has the courage to take a leap of faith, we got there!

When did you hire your first member of staff?

We took on a new member of staff pretty quickly and as I was still doing some hands-on work such as facials we needed a receptionist within the first three months. We then took on another doctor within the first size to nine months, so in the first year we took on three members of staff. We knew that the staff would be a substantial cost but they would also help us grow the business by enabling us to take on more bookings.

Were there any parts of the business that you looked to outsource?

Our doctors get paid for the work they do and aren't employed by us. This works well as some doctors struggle to get business as they have a "doctor's brain" and not a "business brain". They work with us because we can generate clients for them, so they're not having to do anything apart from their job.

How did you know when you could start paying yourself a decent wage?

I believe it is really important in business to pay yourself fairly otherwise you see everyone else earning money and not you. We paid ourselves from day one so we could support our family. We've always paid other people's wages of course but I would also never drop my wages to take on someone else. I would wait until we could afford to pay them and get them generating more money.

What has been your hardest and best year in business so far?

The hardest year was the first year as we were solely focussed on building the business. It's hard to say which has been the best year as there have been so many highs like landing my first column in a newspaper, or getting our dream building, there really have been multiple best years!

Was starting the business and growing it harder or easier than you thought it would be?

I've really enjoyed it so I don't think it has been harder than I thought it would have been. My parents had their own business so I was brought up in that environment. It's been an amazing time, sometimes stretching and stressful, but I've learned so much. Of course we've had tough times, but we have always believed we could get through them.

If you were to start up again now, what would you do differently?

We would have looked at getting investment. I didn't do this when we started because basically, I was a girl from Essex who knew nothing about business or investment. I just made it happen, we simply grew the business organically, we made a bit and reinvested the money back in the business. I don't think there is anything wrong with getting investment to help grow a business.

What are the three most important qualities for an entrepreneur to have?

Tenacity, you really have to stick at it and keep going. **Honesty**, you have to do the right thing by people, I believe doing the right thing comes back to you in the right way and having a sense of **humour** – if you don't laugh, you'll cry!

What has been the best lesson you have learnt in business?

How to manage money. How to make sure that you have money in the right places for when you need it. We have several accounts, all the money goes into one main account and then is split into the others such as tax, wages, rent, etc.

Also, I've learnt how important it is to have regular meetings with staff.

Every week we have a management meeting about finance, projections and things like that. Once a month we have a staff meeting where the team can give feedback, etc. I've also learned the things I'm good at and the things I'm not good at, such as managing people, so now I have people tasked to do the things I am less good at.

What does the next five years look like for you?

We are going to expand. During the lockdown we took on four new people and have more starting in this year. We are expanding into wellness spas and retreats. This was due to a realisation that we can offer people cosmetic surgery but it's no good if the rest of your body is falling apart or you are struggling with your mental wellness. We are going to help people get the latest treatments to de-stress their lives and improve their mental well being as well as their physical health. We had a client in recently with terrible acne, when she asked me what I was going to prescribe her, she was shocked when I said she should start to meditate to bring her stress levels down which was causing her acne, only after that was I willing to move on to the creams.

Aside from setting up our retreats, the first of which is in Suffolk, we are also working on business expansion for the Harley Street Skin brand through the franchising model. In fact, we have several possible franchisees in the pipeline already.

What is your favourite entrepreneurial quote?

The harder you work, the luckier you get!

If you weren't doing this, what would you be doing?

I'd love to have my own range of lotions and potions and natural products. My mother used to make her own skin care products in the 1950s so it's come down the line. She was a huge influence on me.

Do you think you will ever get to the point where you think you've 'made it'?

No! A lot of my friends ask me why I don't just stop and go and lie on a beach. We go away somewhere hot each year after Christmas with the family but I don't ever want to retire. I do four days a week now, and will probably go down to two days a week at some point but why would I want to retire? I love my work!

What is the best bit of business advice you have been given?

The best bit of business advice I have ever been given is from a lady in America who owns a very large skin care business. She is amazing. When I first started, she told me that when you can afford it, get yourself a really good Human Resources person to manage your staff. At the time I didn't understand but as we have got bigger (we have about 50 staff now) it makes perfect sense. The HR person can deal with the staff issues that I can't. Also, my ex-father-in-law once said: "I'll tell you something girl, any fool can work for nothing". This stuck with me and is why we always made sure that we paid ourselves.

What was the most extravagant thing that you bought yourself following business success?

For me it was a house. But for my husband it was a Bentley, then a Porsche and now he's bought an Aston Martin! He works so hard and deserves it. If you see the rewards of your labours it makes all the effort worth it.

LESLEY REYNOLDS

Harleystreetskinclinic.com

48 Harley Street London, W1G 9PU

0207 436 4441

Instagram: @queenofharleystreet

Twitter: @harleystskin

CHAPTER 7

ROGER WOODALL

We are thrilled to share Roger Woodall's (Dodge's) brilliant story with you in this chapter. Dodge is a bit of a local legend in the South of England area, and in the sports and events worlds, and we always get a buzz and a spike in our entrepreneurial energy when we speak to him, as we are sure you will too once you read this. Dodge has a seemingly endless drive and ambition and is a great example of how two things can get you to where you want to be - doing what you love and never giving up.

His approach to business is direct and refreshing, running things like he is the captain of a sports team and his employees are team members, not just staff.

Tell us about who you are and what you do.

I'm Roger Woodall, I've been in the events industry for 20-odd years and my business today is I'm the owner of Bournemouth 7's Festival which is a sports and music festival with 30,000 people partying in a field for three days. I'm also the owner of the Eventful Entrepreneur Podcast and I am also co-host of the Harry Redknapp Show as well as the owner of the Event Crowd which is an online events course which we will be launching in September 2021.

How do you monetise your podcasts?

I get paid to be on the Harry Redknapp Show as the co-host. My personal podcast is a wonderful marketing tool for both businesses, the Event Crowd business and also for Bournemouth 7's. We've just had a sponsor come on board called White Claw which is an American drinks company who now sponsor the whole show.

What were you doing before these businesses?

Bournemouth 7's has been around for the last 14 years, ten years before that I had a student nightclub brand with 12 parties in different cities up and down the country every single week. I ended up putting on 1,500 parties in nightclubs across the UK. I had two brands, one was called Pop Your Cherry and one was Bubble Love.

Have you always been an entrepreneur or have you ever had a "normal job"?

I've never been employed in my life. I've been an entrepreneur since I was ten years old, living in pubs in London where you grow up very quickly. You're around a lot of adults and seeing a lot of businesses and wheeling and dealing going on and that has been my world since a young age.

Why did you decide to start Bournemouth 7's?

It was the next step really for me. I was throwing parties in nightclubs for ten years where I would take the door money and they would take the bar money. I would get 2,000 people in nightclubs every single week from Manchester, London, Brighton, Birmingham to Leicester. The next step was really to move into the festival world where I saw a huge opportunity. The recession had kicked in but this was still an opportunity as there were lots of music festivals happening around the world but no sport and music festivals. Along came the idea of creating a sport and music festival and 14 years on we are still here today.

When you told your wife that you were going to start up the festival, what was her feedback and that of others close to you?

People thought I was mad. They all thought I was absolutely mad. I didn't really listen to them though as I go with my gut feeling. I listen to people who I respect in business, not the people who are just around you. You do get people who are massively supportive who tell you to go for it but you also get the people who seem supportive, but you know they actually think you are wrong for going for it. This was a massive thing and to be honest, I was naive when I jumped into it. Putting events on, putting 10,000 students into parties in nightclubs is very different to putting on a big party in a field for three days. You walk into a nightclub and they have security, they have the bar staff, the bar is stocked, they have toilets, lighting, the DJ box, electricity, they have everything. You go into a field and you have to bring all of that yourself including marquees, tents, policing council licensing, the list goes on.

How did you know where to start?

I knew how to create brands and I knew how to promote. I'm good at marketing and I'm good at selling, so in my eyes any entrepreneur who can do these things is already halfway there. I knew I had all of the tools to throw an amazing party, and let people know about it. This was before social media, meaning the way you could market would be flyers and posters. Flyers went into people's hands and posters went up in cities, everywhere. I had the two worlds of marketing and promoting, I had ten years of 'proper' marketing and promoting, and then Mark Zuckerberg landed on our laps in 2008 and changed everything. I knew I had the contacts, I knew how to throw parties and I was well connected in the sports world with the England Rugby players and other professional sports people around the country, and I had a name back then.

What I didn't know in my naivety was how much it was all going to cost me. I knew I had no staff, it was just myself.

When you got started with Bournemouth 7's, what were your first priorities?

When I first started, I was working from my garage at home which we had turned into an office. We had no staff but there was so much pressure in year one that we had to employ someone. I've always built businesses up before making a move into bigger premises. The biggest killer in business is employing too many staff and taking on big office rent, which I was very aware of, so it took two years to build the business up before we moved into the office we are in now.

I wanted to run it as a lifestyle business and as soon as you employ over ten people, it's no longer a lifestyle business. I run things like I am a captain of a rugby team, we all look after each other, we do everything as a team and this is why we have seen the success we have seen.

You have previously spoken about 19 other businesses you've looked at but decided not to pursue, why is that?

For me, a business must tick eight out of ten boxes before I jump in with both feet. It if only ticks seven, I walk away. I've looked at 19 other businesses over the last 13 or 14 years and to have the strength to say no as an entrepreneur is a wonderful thing. I have seen a lot of friends or acquaintances, people who I mentor, who jump into a business today and really think it is going to work, but if you haven't done your homework fully, you could be stuck in that business for five years and end up losing a lot of money, causing a lot of stress and lack of sleep. 50 per cent of businesses fail in the first 18 months, 80 per cent fail in the first five years and only a very small percentage get past ten years and even then, a lot of them aren't making money.

What are those boxes you look for in a business to tick?

It depends what type of business it is. I looked at Miami Sport and Music Festival and moving over there with the family and creating a multi-sports festival in the US. It ticked quite a few of the boxes, but it didn't tick eight of them. I looked at Cardiff Sport and Music

Festival, and London, but neither could tick all the boxes. I'd go and look at a venue in Cardiff but the car park was too small, not enough pitches, are there too many houses around for example, meaning you can't play music till one o'clock in the morning? All of these things play a huge factor. There are also lots of other businesses I've looked at outside of the events industry such as buying the venue where we host the Bournemouth 7's.

I've realised, having been an entrepreneur for the last 30 years, that it's about having fun and happiness. People often strive to have lots and lots of money, but it's not actually about that, it's about having a successful business that you're happy with and it becomes a lifestyle. I've run all of my businesses with the aim of making them lifestyle businesses, I don't want an empire.

What was the hardest part of setting up the business?

Probably putting my wife through such emotional stress, as we had to remortgage the house in year one of the festival. People didn't buy online back then so we were literally waiting there, on the day of the festival, for people to turn up and pay you money to get in. That was awful.

Remortgaging your home, the house you live in, is fucking crazy and I wouldn't wish having to do that on anyone. I tell the people who I mentor to take calculated risks, and that wasn't calculated. However, I am very happy that I did it as I am now where I am today.

Where there any points when you thought that you had made a mistake with it all?

No, 100 per cent not. Not even when we were £100,000 in to this and had to make the decision to remortgage the house, because as we then found out, with my naivety of not knowing how much a festival would actually cost, that everyone (suppliers) would want their money six months prior to the festival and I had banked on paying them afterwards. That was a massive shock.

How long did it take you to make your first bit of money?

The first festival we did we made £1,000 profit, after a whole year of graft, and stress and pressure and headaches, but also fun and excitement. All of these emotions were thrown into one big bucket, or colander, and all the nice emotions stayed in and all the crap ones fizzled away out of the colander.

It doesn't sound like a lot of money at all, but we knew that an average music festival will take seven years to break even, so we knew we were onto something with the first one making £1,000 profit. We could have easily been £200,000 the wrong way with it and then you lose your house. It was fucking wild. I can't begin to tell you what I put my wife through. I'm cool with risk, but that was a different risk. My wife was in a secure job and had lived in Wales in the beautiful countryside and had never really seen risk, to then meet someone like myself. With the pressures of the whole six months leading up to the first festival, she left her job, a secure job that paid well, and backed my dream. Seeing her cry every time we walked down the beach, or when we would go to bed, that wasn't cool. She had the fear. She was worried but I put on a brave face, it was how it was.

What have you done differently from that first festival to the festival you are putting on this year in 2021?

I now have ten full time staff, I have beautiful offices and we have better systems and structures in place.

In the first year, what was the hardest decision you had to make?

It was the remortgaging of the house. Imagine having to sit down with your partner having already paid £100,000 out with zero left and the only option is to re-mortgage the house in the hope that people will turn up, or in the hope that it's not raining. If it was raining, no one would have turned up and that would have completely ruined the whole thing.

How long did it take for you to decide that you were going to remortgage your house?

I was in straight away, it was the only option. I was 100 per cent in, but then I had to sit down with the Mrs and tell her! That was a difficult conversation, she's very risk adverse. I had to tell her the only option we had was to remortgage the house or we walk away from £100,000 that was already invested and we are left with nothing in the bank and no business. The positive was that we had no kids at the time, that really was the only positive. On the plus side, she thanks me now!

Just to add something onto that, three weeks after that first festival we got married! All of the festival stuff was on top of trying to plan a wedding as well. It was horrible for her. At least we got to spend three weeks in the Maldives on honeymoon after it all happened!

How did you know it was the right time to take on your first member of staff?

I knew it was the right time because when you're in the festival world you're juggling six revenue streams – ticket sales, VIPs, camping, sponsorship, catering and the bar, on top of marketing, designing and promoting. It was just wild. I knew then that I needed help as I couldn't write the emails, go and put the posters up, put flyers out at Twickenham, be in sponsorship meetings, etc., especially when it was all new to me.

I was thinking it would be just like throwing a nightclub party in a field, but it wasn't. You're dealing with fencing companies, WiFi companies, security, police, licensing, marketing, sponsorship, bar, stock, health & safety, Bournemouth airport... the list goes on and on.

Did you outsource any parts of the business?

We kept what we could inhouse but obviously we outsourced certain things like the marquees, lighting, audio and security.

I have always kept sponsorship and bars in house since day one. There's a lot of companies who offer to run the bars for you at festivals and then give the owner a percentage of the bar, but I wanted to keep it in house as the profit can be great.

How did you know how much to pay yourself or reinvest into the business?

I never paid myself. Now I pay myself dividends but I don't pay myself a salary otherwise you can get too comfortable. You never want to be comfortable as an entrepreneur, that's when all things go tits up!

Up until this year, what has been the hardest year in business for you?

Year two of the festival, because I was tweaking and improving things to make people's experiences even more amazing. In year one I was going around looking at everything I could improve for year two and what I didn't know was that the £300,000 cost was going to jump to £450,000, so that put more pressure on to get more people through the door and more people at the bars just to break even. It really was unbelievable pressure.

I didn't realise that when you finish one year, you're straight back into planning for the next one. I thought I was going to have some time off but no, you're right into it again. That brought a lot more pressure in year two as I still had my mortgage money invested which I couldn't take out and pay off, I needed that money again to pay for the next festival, plus even more money. We had to get more sponsors, more people through the doors. The key thing for me is to break even and everything else on top is a bonus. Many entrepreneurs want to start making the money straight away, but as an entrepreneur you get fed last.

What was it that made the costs jump by so much for year two?

More marquees, more party tents, more security, more police, more fencing, more of everything. I didn't want to look at things from the first one and just replicate it and hope to get more people in, because I'm not that way inclined. I want to make an experience for people so when they leave they remember it for the rest of their lives and think it was one of the best weekends of their life. That's why we are coming into year 14 now because that is what we have created each year.

If you were speaking to a new entrepreneur who was just wanting to make a lot of money, would you recommend the events industry for them?

It would really depend on their background. The events world has been my world for 20 plus years. If a young 20-something came to me with no experience but a great business model I would fully back them and advise them they can make a hell of a lot of money in this business if they get it right, but you can also easily lose a lot of money.

Has starting your own business been easier or harder than you thought?

I don't really know as I've never been employed, so I don't know any different. I've always had my own businesses since the age of ten. Since adulthood I have found my niche in the events world and did that for ten years, found a niche in the sportswear world and did that for eight years and sold it in 2018, and now my niche is the festival world. My new niche is going to be moving into the events courses online world and podcasting.

Finding a niche market is key and it's important not to get caught up trying to juggle too many balls and going for new shiny things in business. A lot of entrepreneurs that I see do that, they have one business but straight away start looking at three or four others. Focus on one and become an expert, once you become an expert then you look at doing a few other things.

If you were to start up again today, what, if anything, would you do differently?

Not remortgage the house! Also, not putting my wife through the stress and tears for that first couple of years. Otherwise, nothing really, as the challenges were all valuable learning experiences.

How do you manage your time now?

I just get on and do it. I'm not one of those people who wakes up at 5 am to jog down the stairs to drink a green avocado smoothie before writing down my ten goals I want to do by 7 am. I think that's a load of bollocks. Anyone who does that will do it for a short amount of time. Keep it simple. If you keep business simple, you'll be a success. If you keep life simple, you'll be a success.

What are the three top qualities you think every entrepreneur should have?

1. Keep it simple. 2. Keep it simple. 3. Keep it simple.

I can't express how important this is. If you try to keep it simple it takes a lot of energy and use of your mind to work out how to simplify everything but when you do, everything slots into place.

I just do what I know works well for me, and simplicity for me is the key to happiness. Of course, you do need to be passionate if you want to be successful. We have one life, and life goes very quickly. If you're not waking up every morning and doing something you enjoy, what's the point?

What's the most important lesson you have learned so far in business?

Again, it's just keep it simple but also build a brilliant team around you. Identify what you're good at and what you are good at, become an expert in it. What you're not good at, you don't want to do so get people who are very good at it, it will simplify your life.

What do the next five years look like for you?

Probably the most exciting five years of my life! The reason why I say that is because I really thank Covid and I was super excited when Boris Johnson spoke on 23 March 2020 because I knew what was coming. I lost a truck load of money last year due to Covid because I lost the festival. I knew a global recession was coming because I've been through it and I've set up two businesses in a global recession. I'm grateful because it has driven me to set up my own personal brand and go public with it. Since I launched my podcast and Instagram five months ago and went public with it, so many business opportunities have arrived from so many people I didn't know. I've been having the most amazing conversations with people I would never have had conversations with if it hadn't been for Covid because it made me get my entrepreneur's hat back on. Usually, you spend 362 days a year working on the festival for three days making the money. The last five years it has been such a well-oiled machine that I have been able to step away from the business - I'd have 11 months off and come back for the month of May. If Covid hadn't happened I would still be doing the same. There was a part of me subconsciously itching to get my teeth stuck into something new and Covid made me do this and set up the podcast, the Event Crowd and be part of the Harry Redknapp Show.

What's the most extravagant thing you have bought now you have been successful?

I'm not into fast cars or watches. I love comfort, I love really good food, good company with friends and holidays. Nothing extravagant there, I'm all about the experiences. I spend a lot of time in Barbados, Ibiza, Portugal. That's what I look forward to. I like the simple things in life!

DODGE WOODALL

Website: https://dodgewoodall.com

LinkedIn: https://www.linkedin.com/in/dodgewoodall

Instagram: @dodge.woodall

CHAPTER 8

PAUL ROWLETT

Wow, what a story Paul Rowlett has! We love how this shows that no matter how bad things get and how low you feel, you can always find an opportunity to turn your life around and be successful, you just need to really want to and persevere. Paul's story is by no means a conventional one, there has been drink, drugs, police, hospitals and getting fired from jobs in the past, but he managed to take a new direction, learn a new skill and then turn that into his own successful business. It is never too late, just keep exploring and keep reaching out to people that might be the ones who can help you get there.

Tell us about your business.

In 2010, I launched my first brand within the promotional products industry, supplying pens, bags, mugs and a whole lot more. The ethos is that our products help drive sales, grow awareness, improve engagement and put a smile on faces. We didn't reinvent the wheel, we just do it better. Fast forward 11 years and the business has evolved and expanded, so much so, and through a pandemic, we have rebranded into 'Everything Global' a 360-marketing solutions business. Why? Quite simply we had the resource and space to provide a greater offering to our customers during a difficult time and now beyond. Under the Everything Global brand we now have a digital agency, fulfilment solution, personalised gift house, a community support network and of course Everything Branded. The premise is to provide all customers with the opportunity to use all our services in one simple transaction or account. We think this provides a unique offering and a simple solution to many problems we see on a daily basis.

What were you doing before you set this up?

I was actually kicked out of school pre-GCSEs (or how they put it 'early study leave') that clearly worked as I attained one mighty GCSE in sociology. But regardless I had a plan and in 1999 it was a career in the Royal Navy. However, I soon realised that I didn't really like it, I didn't like taking direction, so I did my time for Queen and Country, serving time in conflict during 'op telic,' which is quite mad to think that I went from that to selling pens now! (My girlfriend goes mad when I say that, because we do sell more than pens!) I was always interested in business, as a kid I used to sell tuck shop sweets and clothes and stuff at school, anything I could make a quid from. When I left the Navy, a friend of mine's dad said, "Why don't you try sales?" because I'd always been a bit of a wheeler dealer, but I'd never been a salesman professionally. So I went into traditional double glazing window sales where I was knocking on doors, doing face-to-face sales in people's houses where you sit there for five hours saying that you're not leaving until you get a deal, that kind of thing. But I was actually quite successful at it, and I did that for about four years until 2007 and I made quite a good living, working when I wanted as it was all commission only. And I have to say that while that industry might have a stigma attached to it, it really was a superb way of learning the psychology of the sales process. Oddly, now over ten years later the guy that was my trainer has actually joined the company as sales auditor, it's weird how the world goes round.

I was fortunate that while in the Navy I managed to buy my first house just before I got into sales, and decided to have people rent rooms from me as well, so I had quite a decent lifestyle back then, with extra money, however when you're living with three lads it's never going to go into savings is it!

Ultimately the sales role had a shelf life as it was late nights and weekends so you do get burnt out, and not many people make it into a long-term career. I got to the point where I needed to move on to something more traditional like business-to-business sales, or tried to, but around that time the financial crash happened and I just went off the rails to be honest as I just could not find a job. I turned to partying way too hard, doing things I shouldn't do, it was a terrible time. It was one of those moments when you take a look at yourself and get a reality check. I'd left a commission only job and I thought that I'd be able to get myself into the corporate world, but unfortunately I was lying to myself - I was a double glazing salesman, I was not a 9-5 corporate guy. So I was going for job interviews at places where I could probably do the job, but they would never hire me.

The realisation that I was just not going to get that stable corporate job, especially when the world was in meltdown, made me slip into really dark days where I was doing too many drugs and drinking heavily and basically sold anything I could to hustle a few quid. I was a complete mess, and one night I had a bit of a cry for help. I remember it now - I was watching Liverpool in the champions league feeling sorry for myself and drank a bottle of vodka, took two boxes of paracetamol and to this day I don't know why, as it was just stupid. But luckily my dad came round, the police came round and I ended up going to hospital for a checkup. I actually remember being in Leicester Royal Infirmary and the doctor said that I can't have taken that many pills, because if I did then I'd be dead, and I was like, "well, I did." It takes a while for Paracetamol to kick in though, and actually I just felt a bit odd, but not like I was dying, so I just pulled all the wires off me and walked out of there and all the way home. The next thing I know is that the police had come back round my house to see if I was OK, my mate James had turned up and that was a turning point for me, because I'd hit absolute rock bottom.

Over the next few days, after a 'hangover from satan', I chatted with my mum and she helped me to buy a suit and encouraged me to go and find a job, so I managed to sort myself out mentally and went for an interview. I did the first interview which went well and I went for the second. It was a BDM role selling Google marketing products like advertising which in 2009 was not as common as today, but one thing this job also offered was a superb fully residential training course to learn the basics of PPC and analytics (which as you read on quite simply changed my life.) It was £28,000 salary job, with a company car and I thought I'd actually made it! I got the job in the end and that was the time that my whole life took a different direction.

However, I was just going from being a 'Del Boy' selling windows and drinking my sorrows away to then putting on a suit and being told what to do by a manager that I knew I was better than. I ended up falling out with her simply because of illogical decisions. To this day I like to make sure none of our team hold meetings for meetings sake, it's just illogical and if you work out the hourly rate of all the people in that meeting, it will make you reconsider if it was that important. One Friday, I was up in Leicester and she was one of these leaders that asked me to go to a meeting at 4 pm all the way over in Birmingham. I told her that was stupid, as it would take 1.5 hours to get there with traffic, we had a massive argument and I ended up throwing my laptop as I had had enough and you guessed it, I got sacked! So after that little escapade I was on the job hunt again. I also met my now ex-wife at that time and moved in with her quite quickly and got a job for an office supplies company where I learnt all about the world of stationery. I took a big pay cut at that place and it was the most demoralising work ever, where I went from being a face-to-face 'closer' of deals in double glazing, then onto a more corporate world of B2B sales, in a suit, in a company car, to then sit on a phone, being told by someone that I've got to do three hours 'talk time' a day for a £16,000 salary. But I have to say the people I worked with at that company were just superb and how the company put emphasis on a great team culture still sticks with me today and something I really champion in our businesses - the power of teamwork and a great fun culture.

As you might guess, this career didn't go on for long either! I went to the office Christmas party and being a big corporation they decided that I had drunk too much that night (I was smashed to be fair, but it was Christmas!) so they put me on suspension, on full pay, and I knew I was getting sacked, so while suspended I managed to find another job selling promotional products. There were about six members of staff, and after only a month or so I was the number one salesman. And while the pay wasn't huge, I could see that I could easily double my earnings from commission - which is where it went all wrong. I did one deal that quite simply changed my life – I sold a job for the NHS which was for 35,000 branded Oyster Card wallets (for travel on the London Underground) which made me around £1,300 commission. But then I took my lunch break and returned for my manager to tell me that sadly that deal was not mine as he had been working on it, so they wouldn't pay me the commission!

We argued and I went home that night and thought, "hold on, why don't I use my knowledge of Google in this industry that I really like, that clearly has loads of repeat business?" (if you understand the importance of great customer service). So right then I decided to take the plunge and rather than cold calling all day, use Google to get people to come to me. Remember back in 2010 Google ads was not what it is now and I also noticed that the competition online was tiny.

I had a problem though, how the hell do I start a business? I literally Googled 'How to start a company'! I registered a company for £15, and at the time I didn't want to do it all on my own because it was a big task, so I asked my mate James to see if he wanted to get involved. His middle name is Alexander and mine's Charles, so we decided to start 'Charles Alexander Distribution' and I deliberately chose a 'generic' business name so we could add more facets later. So we got it started and just three months in it was clear James could not add as much value as planned as his main job was in the USA and he had to go back all the time. So I bought him out of the business, paying him £1,500 which was roughly double what we both put in.

I felt like a big businessman, but in reality I was skint. I'd had my house repossessed, no stable income, but I knew that I could make this work if I got some cash coming in to market the site and upgrade the website. It was just me, in my dressing gown, using a laptop I got free with a mobile phone, and a small whiteboard. I remember my first ever order was for a scaffolding company where I sold them coasters which made me £67. The funny thing was that to land that job it cost me about £50 in Google ad spend, so not the best business model, but it got things going.

Like loads of startups there was no money, but I also had a shocking best personal credit rating, it was that bad I struggled to pay with cash! So it was near impossible to raise capital. My big break came when I sold a job to a farming company. It was a £4,000 order and they paid me half up front which felt like a million pounds back then and the bonus was they didn't need the goods for weeks. So I was a bit naughty and used the money to increase my marketing spend to get the phones ringing.

I was doing everything myself, but I was building my little business, all from a shitty little whiteboard in front of me which had 'invoices to pay' and 'debt to chase' written on it as headers, so I could keep track of everything. Night time was for web development like manually adding SKUs, which was so labour intensive, while also trying to upskill my knowledge of SEO.

I realised I needed to get out of the house and go to a place of work to feel like a business, so I got an office at a place in Leicester, and it was honestly horrendous, with mould in the corners! The building has since been condemned. But I painted some walls and I got myself a bigger white board for the wall above my desk! And I hired my first member of staff, convincing a friend to go self-employed and also at the time we had a lodger at home called Lucy who was a student and I suggested that she came and worked for me part-time too.

Another milestone was when my then wife was getting very upset with her school teaching job, because the system treated her like shit (trust me teachers work hard before people say they get so much time off!), but with her stable income it really gave me the chance to chase my dreams because I didn't have many outgoings, as it was her house I was living in and no real bills coming out - not even car insurance, driving my old Ford Ka which had a dented door.

Sadly the stability was not going to last and after another bad day at school I said, "why don't you just quit?" to which she replied, "I can't just quit because then we'll be in trouble." What happened next was not my proudest moment as I was a bit angry and got drunk, and ended up texting the headmistress (her boss), saying that she'd quit and won't be coming back. You can imagine my ex-wife waking up the next morning and realising what I'd done!

But that was that, and with hindsight it was one of the best decisions ever as she immediately started looking after the admin of the business which gave me space to concentrate on the areas that I was good at - sales and marketing. One tip I would give anyone in business is that you have to step back sometimes and delegate or outsource the roles that are not in your skillset.

In around 2014 we reached another milestone as I had 16 staff members spread over multiple serviced offices. Luckily, a building came up for sale down the road. It was listed for £192,000 and I offered £150,000 because the prices were still trying to recover after the property crash. This place had been on the market forever and so my offer was accepted quickly. We worked from there for about 18 months and then I ended up selling it for over £250,000 and pumped the profit straight back into another office as I needed a bigger one due to now having around 25 staff, but also because I wanted something that would give us a more corporate feel and environment where people would really want to work. So we spent all of that money and more, refurbishing it into a bit of a 'Google-esque' space in line with our creative vibe.

What did friends and family say when you told them that you were going to set your business up?

So remember I had finally managed to get a stable income selling print and promo after being a bit of a "wreck head", so in the eyes of mum and dad I was back on my feet and to then say, "I'm going self employed starting my own business," was never going to go down well. But deep down I think they always knew that I wanted to try to be a businessman. But my Mum, even now, will hear an idea I have and then say "why!?" She has always been content with going to work for somebody else 9-5, get paid, come home and go to bed. I remember saying once that I was forecast to do £250,000 turnover in the first year and she was like "don't get ahead of yourself". It's crazy really but now ten years later £250,000 is not far off my monthly salaries.

When the wheels were in motion with Everything Branded, what were your first priorities?

There were stepping stones in my business journey and one of the first things was getting an office as for me I had to have a 'get up and go to the office mentality'.

The next priority was to get my first member of staff to increase quote output and maintain service levels, as I was getting very busy on my own and there were times customers would call my mobile but I had the number on divert because I was in the post office sending samples, which is just not the best impression for B2B sales.

Enquiries were coming in which was great, but I made loads of mistakes early on even though in 2010 you could simply put adverts up with keywords in and you'll start showing up. But I soon realised that I needed to do 'exact' matches, which means that you'd get more targeted ads but you would need to build more out which with limited budget worked best for me. Down the line I moved to more 'broad' matches, but learned the power of negative keywords, so I could make sure I didn't show up when people searched for words like 'free', as these were not the kind of leads I wanted.

Where was the business coming from then, all through online searches and your website, or were you making outbound calls or using other advertising methods?

I was always chasing enquiries back, because if you don't someone else will, but never had time to do cold calling as I was too busy with inbound leads - from day one, my focus was Google Adwords. A big problem I had though is I didn't know how tracking worked which is so key with any marketing, so I learnt how to do it reading forums mainly.

You've got to bear in mind that it was a lot easier in 2010 compared to 2021, you could literally pay for the Adwords and know that you'd sit at the top of Google when someone searched for 'Promotional products', for example. The problem I had was with a £50 per day budget at £1 cost per click, my competitors realised a cottage business was trying to take real estate so they soon made me burn my budget which is why keyword research is so important as you can find some really good low hanging fruit if you're clever and do your research.

But ultimately either way I needed more budget, but how could I raise money? Simple. Use all my pre-paid money from customers to remarket the business. While this might sound very risky I knew I could sell better than 1 in 3 enquiries so my return was pretty secure if the phone was ringing and by adding more clients faster I would see a big bounce when reorders came back which would be my profit. This way of thinking I maintained for a few years but I always kept our suppliers in the loop of our strategy and ten years later I am sure my transparency is why I still count some of them as my best friends in the world. If you work with suppliers in your business I cannot express how important it is to be transparent, to this day I operate an open door policy as it's a partnership and it should never be just 'them and you'.

Were there any moments once you'd set the business up where you thought that you'd made a mistake and should've stayed in a 9-5 job?

No. Honestly, no. Because I'm quite OCD and have such an addictive personality, I threw myself into the business and was doing 16 hour days every day and spending weekends doing data and adding products, etc. There was never a time when I thought that it was wrong, and in fact it kept me on the straight and narrow and gave me a positive focus - the only way I would've stopped doing it is if I had gone bust.

**If you had gone bust, what would you have done?
Would you have started up something else?**

100 per cent and there have been many times that it was snowballing the wrong way, like selling loads but not getting paid, or extremely bad accounting advice. Now, over ten years later and having now got a great network of some very experienced business friends who I can ask for advice now and then, I am confident of the future and I have a few ideas up my sleeve.

**How long did it take to feel like you'd made
enough money to pay yourself something?**

My first accountant ended up refunding me his fees for about nine months of work, because he didn't actually do anything for me. I was paying him about £300 per month, at a time when I was totally inexperienced and spinning lots of plates, and I found out from friends of friends that he hadn't been doing things right. It got to a point where I had to be a bit strong with him and he admitted that he was in the wrong so paid me back my fees. I suppose when you're a qualified accountant and you could be struck off, it's best not open a can of worms.

So it was in year two when I got the new accountant that I started drawing out small bits of money, but it was bare minimum and wasn't a regular salary or anything. When my ex-wife joined the business from her teaching job, she organised all the crazy admin and added structure so we could start paying ourselves.

**Since 2010 when you started up, what has been
the hardest decision you have had to make?**

I think many business owners went through this in 2020, it was all down to the COVID-19 pandemic. We had to let people go without any idea if we would be able to rehire them again, or if the company would even survive! We had just set up an office in Las Vegas and committed to six figures worth of refurb costs all based on overwhelming demand and our plans to settle there. But then uncertainty started and the border was about to close which meant my training team had to leave, so we had to temporarily shut the doors as it was not sustainable. What made it worse is that the UK was six weeks ahead of the USA when it came to the virus, so you can imagine my reasons for shutting made no sense to them and it was all done over the phone, which I would never do in normal times. The Vegas office remained closed until May 2021 and at time of writing we are back up to 11 sales people and a local manager, but the cost has been at least $500k, and that's conservative. Sadly this story was replicated in the UK where I had to lay off over 40 people (pre-furlough) in a matter of days after seeing a 97 per cent drop in demand and over £500,000 in cancellations, because we supply events and expos.

What mistakes have you made along the way?

One of my biggest mistakes was in 2014 when I leased an office without planning ahead enough to understand how quickly we would outgrow it - this happened in about nine months. Even now, in 2021, I'm still paying the lease!

My second biggest mistake was trying to get into franchising. It probably cost us £30,000 in time to build a franchise model, which at the time we couldn't afford. We were going to launch it with a brand called 'UK Print Warehouse', where our central office would generate enquiries and fire them out to franchised territories. It was the managing of people and their expectations that was the problem. If you are a franchisee with one of our territories, and you've paid say £10,000 to be one, but for whatever reason the central office doesn't manage to send you as many enquiries as expected, then you're understandably going to kick off and I could see the people would be the problem here. Oddly now with such a good team and resources we could probably make this work but I have told myself never spread yourself too thinly as we have a clear plan to follow currently with Australia expansion and grow USA.

Hindsight is of course a wonderful thing, but looking back, some of the people that I hired weren't right, such as friends of friends, who had no experience or skills really, but thought that they could pick the phone up and sell, when they actually couldn't. Another example of me getting a bit carried away and running before I walked. It was silly 'vanity rather than sanity' at times!

When Did You Know it was right to take on your first member of staff?

Simply that there was too much work. Cashflow was tight then, but the enquiries were flying in so I didn't want to miss any. But it was scary because I went from me and my laptop at home, to £300 a month for a small office and £1,000 a month for another salary, plus commission. It was the best thing I ever did in the business though, because I wanted to grow. Bringing Ross in was more down to the fact that we were friends to be honest! I'd known him a long time, we'd worked together before and I knew that he'd do a great job.

What parts of the business, if any, did you outsource?

In the early days, the suppliers helped us out a bit with the design of products. We would also outsource to a Google partner once the growth happened, because that became too busy for me to manage anymore, along with everything else. I looked at a Virtual Assistant for a while, but that didn't work out because it actually became too much hassle to keep speaking with them - you might as well do it yourself.

Are you able to pick out the best and worst years of business so far?

Actually, the best was last year, 2020, for me as a business owner. Which I know sounds crazy after sharing such misery early on. But it made me step back and reflect on the business which we now do more often and find ways to create other revenue streams, and they were staring me right in the face. Everythingfulfillment.com and Everythingdigital.com have been successful, as we had space to monetise, plus we have been doing digital marketing for ten years with a great team. The digital marketing part will easily add £500k of revenue in 2022 using existing staff, which is very profitable but also adds great value to our customers who want a full marketing solution and one invoice. I'm very proud of these decisions.

Everything Fulfilment was a no-brainer as we had space and suddenly people were all working from home so we started asking customers if we could help them with any of their fulfilment needs. And happily we are now being paid to store and dispatch on request, which not only generates extra revenue but when you add convenience into a buying decision then would you bother leaving for a competitor?

The most exciting time in the last ten years was the first time we launched the American business. We were in the UK office late at night, having spent six months building the website, adwords and adding products, etc, and we went live with Google and watched those visitors land. However, for a week or so we could not realise why the visitors were not converting. We were spending literally thousands to get the data and it was such a simple reason, the data that we were getting from the US suppliers was the RRP of each product, compared with the UK supplier data always being the *cost* price for each item. So we were advertising the American products with added margin, which made us WAY too expensive! But once we'd sorted it out and it kicked in, seeing those first proper enquiries was really exciting.

But for all the positives of 2020 it was also the worst year business wise. In March 2020 the entire country was in meltdown! I was in tears worrying that I might lose everything. I had an office in the USA I could not even visit so actually we had the best and the worst in one year - it's stupid!

Was starting your own business easier or harder than you thought?

Actually neither, I just found it exciting. Hard work didn't scare me, and when I was in the Navy I served in conflict and hardly slept for weeks, so spending hours and hours building my business wasn't an issue. I had always wanted to be able to say that I've got my own proper business and the way that I've done it is by living and breathing it, which I still do.

If you were to start again today, what, if anything, would you do differently?

Get a good accountant straight away. It sounds like a bit of a boring answer, but in my business and life in general, I need someone to reign me in! I'm a very risk vs reward kind of person, I always look at the good in opportunities, but these days I base my decisions more on data than my gut. A good and experienced accountant is the person who helps you to make sensible decisions and can manage the growth for you. Secondly I'd probably embrace outsourcing better. Back in 2010 there was not the tech support that we have nowadays so if I was starting starting a business now, I would maximise what support is out there, as remember with an outsource partner you can pick up and put down but with a person it's a lot harder. However I would say you can outgrow outsourcing so it's not a long-term fix but great to get started and prove concept.

How do you manage your time, splitting work and personal life?

Well in the past I didn't, I was too hands-on, and also with the birth of my daughter it does make you look at your work life balance more. Even so I do still get caught up in things, I remember only recently I checked LinkedIn and this guy had called me and the company out publicly with a picture of a damaged product, saying, "Maybe you can sort it out", because he knew it was my business.

I didn't mind and said on his post that I commend him for calling me out publicly and I did all of the customer service journey openly, as I love being transparent and let's be straight. How do you really know a good business by a perfect delivery? I would argue you only know a business is great if they rectify problems which is what we do and why we are so passionate about online reviews which help not only praise our team but also improve our failings. The annoying thing with this complaint was that the boxes were damaged when they arrived, and we are not a courier company, so it wasn't technically our fault, but it's important to take responsibility and sort things out quickly anyway.

I don't really switch off though and I'm on my phone a lot at different times of the day as our American office finishes work sometimes past 1 am UK time, due to the time difference, so it can be video calls at midnight.

What are the three most important qualities that you think an entrepreneur should have?

Delegation – if you do not delegate as you grow you will hinder your team's personal development and whether you like it or not the number two reason for someone staying in a role is progression opportunities so you have to let go at some point or it will cost you long-term.

Listening - although I've always been terrible at it, I am getting better and trying harder!

Confidence/positivity – even though there were times during the pandemic that I lost it, I would say that a great attribute is to be confident under pressure and to not be negative around the team as negativity is a virus in some offices and will spread fast and you being the leader have to always see the good in a situation.

What does the next five years look like for you?

In five years we will be 16 years old, so by then we may have a strategic partner involved to take the brand even further but if not I would like to think we would add a few more key senior roles to the team, however the focus for me is to prove our model in a few more countries first which is something we are actively working on. From a personal view I'm already very proud that I look after my mum and dad a bit financially. As I grew up with fuck all, mum was a receptionist and dad was a painter, so it's really nice to be able to help them out now. But most of all I want to be a great dad.

What is your favourite entrepreneur quote?

I very much agree with Richard Branson's mantra of 'screw it, just do it'. I hate meetings where you have them just to agree on the next meeting. Indecision slows progress, I am not as rash with decisions these days because I have a great FD, but I still follow a 'risk and reward' philosophy and if the reward is big enough then why not?

EVERYTHING GL🌐BAL
EMBRACE THE POWER OF EVERYTHING

Founder of Everythingglobal.com
in Paul Rowlett

EVERYTHING BRANDED
THE ULTIMATE IN
PROMOTIONAL PRODUCTS

EVERYTHING COMMUNITY
WITH A COMMUNITY WE
HAVE EVERYTHING

EVERYTHING DIGITAL
A CREATIVE POWERHOUSE
OF MARKETING

EVERYTHING FULFILMENT
SAVE TIME AND MONEY
CHOOSE FULFILMENT

EVERYTHING PRINTED
GIFTS FOR MAKING
MOMENTS MATTER

EVERYTHING GL🌐BAL
SEE HOW WE
EMPOWER OTHERS

CHAPTER 9

ASMIR BEGOVIC

What a down to earth and switched on guy Asmir Begovic is. He has a long, successful professional football career but knows that it won't last forever, which is why it's so interesting to hear how he looks to the future. Asmir created his business to play on his strengths and experience as a pro athlete and to ensure that he can remain in the football world that he loves. He knew what he wanted to create and surrounded himself with a team of people to get everything in motion - a key factor in any side hustle, when you are so busy that you have to work smart with your time and not be too precious about wanting to hold and manage every little piece of the business. We love Asmir's mantra in a difficult situation: "take that negative experience and use it as fuel to prove them wrong".

Can you give us an introduction to your main 9-5 and also your side hustle?

My main job is being a professional footballer. It's a profession I have had now for many, many years. It was always my dream to be a professional goalkeeper and thankfully I've never had to look at plan B. Goalkeeping is in my family as far back as my grandfather and it's something I am very passionate about, which led me onto the Asmir Begovic goalkeeping businesses which are part of my long-term plan with my immediate focus very much on playing as long as I can. The

AB1GK business is something I want to grow, developing some of the world's best goalkeeping products and keep on connecting with the goalkeeping community.

What was your knowledge like of the goalkeeping products market and the competition already operating in it?

It's interesting as my passion for goalkeeping started many years ago but I started thinking about goalkeeper gloves as a business probably when I was turning 30 a couple of years ago, when I was looking to the future and thinking about what I could do with my life post-football. At the time I was in a bit of a bad place with my sponsors and was setting up my goalkeeping academy in Bosnia. Myself and my business partner looked into the market to identify what we thought was missing and there wasn't really anyone doing personalised goalkeeper gloves as a professional athlete and goalkeeper. We thought there was a market for this so started looking at other sports where people identify with athletes. I know it's at a much higher level but if you look at the Michael Jordan Brand, or LeBron with Nike, or Tiger Woods with Nike, people very much seemed to associate with the athletes rather than the brand, which we thought was really interesting.

Do you feel it is a necessity to be passionate about the product or service you are doing as your side hustle?

From my point of view, it absolutely helps. I've realised that through playing football, it has been something I have wanted to do basically since I was born so it's never really been a job for me as it has been my passion. I think it makes it a lot more enjoyable as well if it's your passion and therefore easier to put the work in. I've got my name on my products which comes with the added level of pressure but also helps you when it comes to being passionate about it.

Would you have considered setting up your side hustle by yourself, or was it always something you were going to do with a team around you?

One of the key things that I knew right away, before I got the business to what I call a serious level, was to surround myself with people who were experienced and knew what they were doing. I already had a small team around me before, but to really launch the range of gloves and launch this brand into a couple of ranges I knew I had to bring in the right people who had done this before at the highest level. The first people who got involved were the MD and product designer and these two people, along with the team I had already, I felt were crucial to launching the business. We meet regularly to discuss everything related to the business.

It was important to have this team around me straight away as I still play football and am incredibly focused and motivated to keep doing this as my day job, so needed people from day one who I could trust to help me launch.

What was the driver for setting up the side hustle business?

There was a short, medium and long term vision. I was thinking about what would happen after football but also how I want things to look now and in five years time. We definitely saw a gap in the market and we thought this was something that hadn't been done before. People who would buy our products would relate to goalkeepers and our brand was starting to be powered by goalkeepers. We were giving goalkeepers a voice and also an opportunity to wear goalkeeper-driven products. Normally the products are part of a global brand and almost an afterthought. In terms of the longer-term plan, which was another driver for setting up the business, I was thinking what is going to happen after football and thought this was a business I want to drive forward. In the short and medium term, I thought it was important to start this business whilst I was still relevant in the game as this would give the brand credibility. If at the highest level I can trust this product, that will go a long way to reassuring people that it can be worn at any level.

Was it a simple decision for you to start something up on the side of your professional career or did you take a lot of time to consider it?

It definitely took a bit of time. My biggest concern was I had a vision of how it should work, but knew I had to have the right people involved and people who were going to share my same level of passion. I knew I couldn't do it by myself, I knew my limitations and my time restraints, and although I would have final say on the important things, I still needed someone to run it on a day-to-day basis. That process took a little bit of time and I wanted to get it right and take my time rather than rushing and starting something incorrectly just because I saw a gap. It was crucial for me to build up the foundations and build them as strong as possible to give us the best possible chance of making this successful.

What advice would you give someone on what to do and what not to do when starting up their own venture or side hustle?

I would advise someone that they should have a passion about something, surround yourselves with the right people and make sure you enjoy working with them. I would also advise them to have patience, the numbers won't look great at the start but they get better and you need to have that long term vision. Don't give up, get your short, medium and long term vision and celebrate each milestone. Also, an obvious one is to understand that not everyone is going to be a fan of what you do, you will get the negative criticism and sometimes you do have to swallow your pride and ego and listen to it to understand what people are saying they want from your product or service.

How do you deal with any negative criticism both on the pitch and with the business?

When I started as a professional footballer did the negative criticism and comments affect me? Of course they did. Do they now? No. You learn in that environment to get thick skin quickly. This is one area where being an athlete has helped prepare me for the business world because you develop that strong resilience and learn to live with it. There is no way of learning how to deal with it unless you go through it. There will be some negativity around what you are doing which will have no substance to it at all, which you can ignore and then some which will be constructive which you can take on board.

What transferable skills do you have from one role to another?

Resilience is the main one. When I was younger and told people I wanted to be a professional football player, people would tell me I was delusional, but I was determined. I have taken this resilience into the business world and have been very glad I did.

How do you stop a bad day on one role affecting you in the other and keep the two worlds separate?

It comes down to perspective for me and understanding. I can now categorise my family's position in my life, football and the side hustle. Also, making time for other things such as charity work helps me put more perspective into it. This helps fit it all in as well as enabling me to put more energy into everything.

What was the hardest part of setting up your side hustle?

The first part where we were putting the team together. It took a lot of time and it was crucial that we got it right and that everyone believed in what we were doing. In the early days the retailers didn't necessarily believe in what we were doing, they had to see more proof and see more goalkeepers wearing the gloves to help show that this was something we were serious about and it wasn't just a short-term thing. I had thought that it would be relatively easy to get into retailers but I had to prove myself again. I had proven myself on the pitch for many years but had I proven myself in the business world? No, I hadn't. I was asking myself why this wasn't coming as easily as I had hoped and essentially had to go back to scratch and deal with some of the negative feedback.

Every day now it's a new challenge to prove myself and show that I am worthy of what we are doing. If we rest on our laurels then we will never achieve the success that we want to.

How long were you working on this before you launched it into the market?

I started selling some merchandise and developing my brand in 2015. From the time we got the team assembled to the point that I launched my first goalkeeper glove collections was probably nine months or so but it took the best part of six years of conversation before this to get to this stage.

We almost talked it into existence. We talked about whether we could do it, is this just a dream or is it actually possible? But when you do see an opportunity, I think it is important that you are able to pounce and make it happen in a quick way.

I believed that we should start small, but let's start incredibly strong, make sure the team is right and the quality is good. It may not be 100 per cent where we want it to be but keep the core principles around where we want it to be and then we can let it grow.

What would you tell someone who is looking to start up about the first thing they should be doing or thinking about?

I think really it's to learn to walk before you can run. Focus on one or two products, we started with just two products and made sure we did them really well, we wanted them to pop to people and get it out there and grow it that way. Start small, start right, don't overstretch yourself too soon or things will spiral out of control. We have to start somewhere but start in the right way.

What did friends and family say when you told them about the side hustle?

My family has the same belief as me which is to always dream big, don't have any regrets and do it, so they were really supportive. I had this with my football career as well, I left high school to pursue my dream in England, it was a once in a lifetime chance so I took it and it paid off.

Do you think there is an optimum amount of side hustles you should aim to have?

I don't know if there is an optimum number to have, but again I think it is important to dream big but understand your limitations as well. I know how much time and energy football takes from me and how much time and energy it takes to be a husband and dad and to try and be an entrepreneur as well takes a lot. You do have to know limitations and by starting small you can manage this. I also think when you're older you are aware of what you can do and what you can't do whereas when you're younger you think you can take on the world, and often you can but still be aware.

When you have finished playing football, do you think your focus will remain with AB1K or look for other projects as well?

I am always open minded to opportunities. I think something the last year has taught us with the pandemic is not to try and predict too much what's round the corner. There are always plans for the short, medium and long term vision but I try not to predict what will happen. I have a lot of options whether it's football, running AB1K, coaching with my academy, TV work. I am open minded and always want to learn and get involved in different things and then if I find something I want to commit to I will give it as much energy and time as I can.

What has been the best and worst day or year in business so far?

The best was probably when I signed for AC Milan, they are one of the giants of football and getting pictured in my gloves wearing that kit was pretty cool. The worst period was probably when my football career was a little up in the air, I wasn't playing and wasn't really involved with the team and a couple of retailers were questioning how good my product was because I wasn't in the first team. When people doubt you, or put a bit of disrespect on what you do, you can take that negative experience and use it as fuel to prove them wrong. What's funny is those same retailers are now doing five figures a month with us!

What do the next five years look like for you?

I think they look very promising for us. We have a new flagship range we want to keep developing and also add to. We want to grow the products as much as we can and keep disrupting the goalkeeper market and be one of the best-known brands in the world, there is no doubt about it. We're making some big moves already with the keepers and people we are signing and the numbers and customers we have.

What's been the best bit of business advice you've received?

The two that have stuck with me, as I have already talked about, are to start off small and don't overstretch yourselves and the second one for me is don't be afraid to fail. What that truly means we might never know, but reach out there and draw as many people as you can into your product, be as expressive as you can and don't be afraid of the consequences. The fear of failure can help channel your product and no one wants to fail but if you don't try anything you will hold your business back.

What do you think the key to your success in business has been?

The key has probably been having the passion, drive and vision to execute what I wanted to and the belief in myself, my team and my product. I think that having a positive state of mind is really important to everyone.

If you had to start up the side hustle again, what, if anything, would you do differently?

Overall, I have been incredibly pleased with what we have accomplished, but I probably could have been a little more direct in terms of our marketing and getting the product out there. As much as I believed in what we were doing I was a little bit hesitant and shy in questioning myself whether people would actually want to wear my gloves, so I probably could have been a little bit braver in getting it out there sooner.

What's the best thing about having a 9-5 and a side hustle?

It's probably taking me away from the pressures of being on the field. It's a different kind of pressure, it's running my own brand in a different environment and it's refreshing and humbling to be around the goalkeeper community.

ASMIR BEGOVIC

Instagram: @asmir1 @ab1gk @abgkacademy @theglovebank

Twitter: @asmir1 @ab1gk @abgkacademy

Websites: https://ab1gk.com
https://www.asmirbegovicfoundation.com

CHAPTER 10

CRAIG WILLIAMS

Craig Williams is another excellent example of having the courage to take the leap and follow your passion. Craig had a well paid job as an oil broker for many years, but ended up turning a passion for supercars into the next step in his career. Craig became part of an existing business and with his business partner worked to grow it into the world's largest private members supercar club. Most days Craig is in or around some of the world's most amazing and desirable supercars and hypercars and that sounds like a very good use of time to us!

Tell us about your business:

Auto Vivendi is a private members club and we provide our members convenient (and financially astute) access to our collection of supercars which is constantly evolving.

Now in our 16th year, we rebranded in 2013 as a conscious move away from supercar clubs of old and to make membership more around the supercar lifestyle and the enjoyment of driving rather than talking about camshafts and 0-60 times!

What were you doing before you joined Auto Vivendi?

I was an oil broker. I left university and became a bar manager of a tennis-themed bar in Wimbledon village called 'Volleys'. I went through a series of jobs, as many people do when they leave university, mainly in advertising sales which actually gave me a great grounding for what I ended up doing. I bought a business that had gone bust and was going to set it up as a marketing consultancy as that is what I had done my degree in. On the day I was leaving with all of the kit and stock I had bought I got a call from a friend who was an oil broker in Mayfair who told me about a position as a Junior Broker and asked if I was interested in it. I advised him that I was literally in the car about to drive to Wales to start this business but he said I really should go and see them, so instead of driving to Wales I ended up driving to Mayfair! I started as a Junior Oil Broker and worked my way up the ranks and ended up being an Oil Broker for the next 18 years, across a couple of different companies.

That's where I really cut my teeth in terms of learning about financial markets and entertaining successful people, albeit in the oil market lots of them were trickier than they are in the luxury lifestyle market.

Whilst I was an oil broker I had a hobby that actually turned into a business called 'VMAX 200' which is a top speed event that offers people the chance to bring their own cars and drive them at 200mph on an airfield. I set that up essentially as a fun thing for me and my mates along with my brother and it just grew and grew. To cut a long story short, I got introduced to my now business partner who called me one day needing to borrow a Lamborghini Aventador for an event they were running and he had been let down for the car. I managed to find him one and he suggested that we meet up for something to eat and when we did we really hit it off – we had the same ideals about what we were going to do, and what we wanted to accomplish with our brands.

What were your reasons for leaving the job as an Oil Broker to join Auto Vivendi as a Director?

Sadly, my older brother passed away and that gave me the impetus to really reassess what was important to me. I realised what was important to me wasn't the stress of looking at a screen of numbers and screaming down phones. I was a very different person when I was brokering in some respects, I was very volatile and snappy and was renowned for smashing the dealer board when deals went wrong. I realised that I had probably had my time doing that and whilst it was financially very rewarding, it wasn't in any other way in the end. I became part of Auto Vivendi as a Director and shareholder and instantly gave myself a massive pay cut, so it was a big decision to make and one I discussed at length with my wife because clearly initially it was going to change our lives.

When you joined Auto Vivendi, what was the first thing you did?

I didn't really have to change too much. I had known about the club in its previous entity and actually nearly joined years before, but the mindset of the consumer then was very different and I liken it to CD's - when CD's came out everyone wanted in their living room a big hi-fi and then a stack of 200 CD's next to it. If someone had said you can get all these songs on your phone and essentially borrow them most people probably wouldn't have wanted them even though it was way easier. You would have wanted people to see all those CD's. In the same way back then, most people, myself included, would have wanted that status of a supercar sat on their drive, it meant something to you. As time has evolved, and something we are particularly finding with newer, younger members, they don't feel the need to own their own supercar and prefer to just be able to dip in and out of access whenever they want.

So, when I joined, I didn't really change too much as I knew the club and liked it. I knew my now business partner and we were very much on the same page. I wanted to come in and focus on the events side and see what value I could add to them and make them better and safer in the case of the higher speed events.

What is the main reason for your members joining and staying with the club and how important is it to know the reasons?

It's really important. We have people who join, and tell us they joined as they are mainly interested in the events. They buy a big, chunky membership, we show them the events and they don't come on any of them and they end up using their membership purely for the cars.

Generally, no matter what reason they give, the real reason is the cars. Most of our members either own, or have owned, supercars so they understand that as an owner you will go out and buy a supercar, which costs a chunk of change, and instantly you'll take a hit on depreciation, you have to insure it, you have to service it a year later, put tyres on it and all those other things, and that's an expensive business. We always say we aren't there to replace ownership, we want people to buy the supercar they like, and they often buy them through us in fact, but we are there to enhance and compliment their ownership.

When you told friends and family you were leaving your job to join Auto Vivendi as a Director and Shareholder, what did they say?

They were actually all very supportive, all of them, I was very lucky. For my wife, she was very much stepping into the unknown but she knew my life was very stressful and I wasn't all that happy doing the brokering. They were interested and excited, but if they hadn't have been, I would have listened to their points and considered them, and then I would have done it anyway!

When you joined, what were your first priorities?

The immediate thing was to look at our social media. Our website had recently been done but we set the social media side on fire and turned that up as much as we could. We didn't want to go down the line of buying likes and buying followers though, we just grew organically. We had a good team of people and were pretty brand aware and knew what we wanted to represent.

Along with the social media we focused on marketing and we actually did a promotion where new members with a certain membership got a free Hublot watch worth £11,000. That drove interest nuts for a little bit and was really popular. A few weeks after this we did our 'Geneva by private jet' trip which is always really popular – we went to the Geneva motor show by jet and we did a big photoshoot around this. We really started to tell people in a much bigger way about who we were and what we did. We had tried a lot of different advertising in different ways, some of it really didn't work like ads in the *Telegraph* and *Financial Times*.

How important is social media to your business?

It's a bit of a shop window for us. Our following wasn't really something we chased and we grew it organically until Gareth Bale joined the club! When he joined, watching the Facebook likes come in was amazing. So yes, it is important to us as a shop window although not too many of our social media viewers are potential members yet but they will be. The interesting thing is we've had a lot of people say to us that when they make their first million, or sell their business, they want to join Auto Vivendi which is a huge compliment as historically what normally follows is them saying they want to buy a Ferrari.

What was the hardest thing about joining an established business as a Director and Shareholder, how did you make your mark on it?

The hardest bit, which I never really understood at the start, was what it was like to run a small business - like understanding how important cash flow is and how you may need to look at a strategy to drive cash flow at a certain time. I remember a financially astute member advised us that you can only run out of cash once, and that is really true in business.

In terms of making a mark, I did that by driving the social media, or putting on cool and exciting events. An example of this was when we put the holy trinity of hypercars against each other - the McLaren P1, Ferrari LaFerrari and Porsche 918 Spyder - and invited people to come and drive them at 200 mph. By doing events like this it was really putting a marker in the sand to a lot of people about the kind of level we operated at.

Did you have any moments when you thought you had made a mistake leaving the security of the day job?

No, I didn't have any moments where I thought I had made a mistake at any point, but I did have moments where shortly after starting I got offered a couple of pretty big punchy jobs in oil brokering and did I consider them for five minutes or so, of course you couldn't not have, but I never really thought I had made a mistake.

I was pretty confident with my decision and happy with it once I started. It's a bit of the old Yin-Yang type of thing, my business partner and I both clown around a lot but we also take the business really seriously and we have the perfect attributes to mirror each other. Things like that really help to reaffirm my decision.

What happens when there is a disagreement at work between you and your business partner, how do you deal with that?

We haven't ever really had a major disagreement about anything big because generally we think along the same kind of lines. There are times when we tell each other if we disagree on something but we will always try and work it out like grown ups do. The few times when we have lost the plot and screamed at each other, within ten minutes we are laughing about it, we know it's not personal, it's business. Very rarely do we have disagreements about the business and when we do we are very good at articulating what we believe. We can sometimes go back and forth on something and we've ended up doing something that wasn't the right thing to do and then we have discussed it so we know for next time. I am not afraid to say that I have made some mistakes, every business person has. You have to be big enough to admit it and chalk it up to experience.

What, if any, part of the business have you outsourced?

We are able to do most things in house and have become quite adept at turning our hands to different things, particularly during lockdown when we have had to. We outsource things like film making, we do have a filmmaker in house but when we really need to do something bigger we have a few people we can call on. If we are going to do a lot of targeted social media we have an agency we can use to work on that although a lot of it we do ourselves. The majority of things we try and keep in house if we can.

What has been the best and worst year of business so far for you?

The best year was probably 2019, although we were all set to have a great 2020 but obviously Covid put a stop to that. Whilst it was a challenging year with cancelling events and things like that it could have been a lot worse. The events we put on in 2019 were really good and included sponsorship from Aston Martin, we met some great people and it was an all round great year for us.

2020 was tough for everyone, it took its toll on us without a shadow of a doubt as a small business, we have bills to pay and as you can imagine we have quite high fixed costs.

Was the experience of joining a company and helping build it harder or easier than you thought it would be?

Harder. It was a very established business which had been running for a long time but before I got involved there was a lot of unstructured debt in the business which we paid off because we knew that the supercar industry couldn't handle a business like ours going under or screwing people over and then starting up again so we made sure we paid it off.

It was harder than I thought it would be also from the point of view that it was a lot more involved then I realised. In many ways even now if we look at the crawl, walk, run analogy, even going into our 16th year with a better collection of cars than we have ever had, and with money in the bank, we still feel like we are just starting to walk.

If you were to start up again today, what if anything, would you do differently?

Although I haven't been involved for the whole 16 years, in many ways the last 16 years has been an evolutionary curve of learning and understanding the consumer. The historical model of the supercar club industry was run by people who wanted to turn their own cars into an industry and/or their customers were people who were never really going to be able to afford the cars and as such that wasn't a predictable or sustainable business, and one which was very hard to plan for. If anything happened in those people's lives, the first thing to go was their supercar club membership. We have evolved that model and amended our prices to ensure that our members are able to afford it. Although it's a considered and discretionary spend for them, their membership cost isn't changing their world dramatically.

I don't think I would have changed anything as this has been an evolutionary learning curve which has got us to where we are today.

The main thing we have changed is the business model, previously we did it on points, now you get miles and days in cars. It was the main reason I didn't join the club originally as I didn't understand it, I thought there was some sort of catch I was missing. We looked at our membership model and thought we had to get it as near as we can to the ownership experience, and one thing that people who own supercars understand is roughly how many days they use them and how many miles they want to drive. If we can tell them exactly what that is going to cost them, it will change our world, and it has. It was a bit of an epiphany moment early last year.

How do you manage the work life balance?

I'm in an interesting place because of what I do. It's many people's dream to fly on private jets or drive supercars. We can get calls from someone saying can I land my jet whilst you do one of your events and we'll end up having a race between a jet and a car, it's really crazy! I am very fortunate and I am aware of how fortunate I am getting to do some of the stuff I do and as such it does mean that I'm not in a position where I am constantly chasing the next holiday or time off. People do see this side on social media but don't see the times we are up at two in the morning trying to put an event together, or when a member says they are bringing in someone and it's been five days since the cleaner has been in so I'll be there scrubbing the toilets!

Last year was obviously different. Where I would normally be travelling for 60-70 days of the year, I barely left the house, but even with that I do need to try and leave the office a little bit earlier. It's very easy to sit there working away on a Friday night and suddenly it's 9 pm, but on a weekend for example I make sure I spend it with my family, so overall I have a pretty good work life balance.

What are the top three qualities an entrepreneur needs to have in order to be successful?

I think resilience is important, you need to be able to take the rough with the smooth and realise that it's not going to be all wins.

The second one I think is to learn to celebrate the little wins. I'm a terrible one for just looking at the end result and thinking when we have done (this) we will have (this). But sometimes you have to enjoy the ride and not just be thinking about the next thing. Lastly, organisation. You have to be organised both in terms of the little things and the big things. You have to be on it all the time and not take your eye off the ball.

CRAIG WILLIAMS

Website: https://www.autovivendi.com/

Instagram: @Auto_Vivendi / @craig_auto_vivendi

CHAPTER 11

NICHOLAS FRANKL

What an incredible person Nicholas Frankl is - it's not everyday that you get to speak with a three-times Olympian, pilot, humanitarian, investor, writer/test driver and thrower of exclusive HNWI (High Net Worth Individuals) yacht parties!

We learned so much in our conversations with Nicholas and they gave us a real feeling that anything is possible if you put yourself out there and start asking questions.

We also love his personal tagline: 'Connecting the world's most interesting people'.

Can you tell us a little about your business ventures?

I've been a serial entrepreneur my whole life. I can't remember the first time that I thought about business, because I can't remember a time when I didn't think about business, or about creating something, starting something.

One of my earliest experiences was when there was a chance to create a bobsled team, with the goal of trying to reach the Olympic Games in just 12 months. This was of course quite a sizeable challenge for someone that had never seen a bobsled, let alone done the sport! But we prevailed, with thanks to my father Andrew, who has been a tremendous and overriding influence in my life, and we created the first Hungarian bobsled team in the winter of 1992, our first race was in January 1993 and we qualified to compete in the Lillehammer Olympics by February of 1994, and I was just 23 years old.

Why did you want to get into the entrepreneur world, rather than getting a regular 9-5 job?

If you're given the opportunity to get an amazing 9-5 job, which is well paid and you're doing something that you love, then of course that's not a bad option, and I certainly looked at that. You look at everything when you're young, you don't necessarily know which direction you're going in, but I was always exposed to motor racing and I spent my youth growing up around Formula 1, again thanks to my father, so I was always around commercial teams and sponsors. In fact, I remember my old history teacher saying "Frankl, I don't have to worry about you eating - you'd be able to sell ice to Eskimos". And I've been selling 'ice to Eskimos' my whole life since then.

I had a careers discussion at my school when I was about 18 years old, and the careers advisor said to me, "I think you should be the next Terry Wogan - you should be a television personality", and I thought that sounds like a good idea, so I tried to get into television. I knocked on doors and ended up presenting on Sky TV, I called up BBC South in Guildford and said that I'd like to talk to them about Formula 1, because there were two Surrey-based teams, McLaren and Tyrell, at the time, and they said, "Great! We'll pay you £10 per segment". This was a good lesson in fragility, because it cost me a lot more on the telephone to call in the reports than the £10 that I received!

But it got me on the air and when I was on the BBC they said, "Well, you're quite good at this, so why don't you do Wimbledon for us?", so then I ended up commentating there in 1991, aged 22 or something, watching Jeremy Bates on centre court and with a media pass and access to the player room, etc. You never know where these things will lead, so you've got to get on with it. You've got to get off your arse because fortune favours the brave and so does luck. I think that 'lucky' people are those that seek out the luck. That is going to help you as an entrepreneur, you never know where the world is going to take you or where the opportunities are going to come.

These days you are well known for being the CEO of My Yacht Group, how did that start and what was the key driver for starting it up?

I was hired in 1996 by Edward Asprey when they were looking for a Formula 1 team sponsorship manager and Asprey, which is the Queen's jeweller from Bond Street in London, a 250 year-old brand and the holders of four Royal Warrants, had just been purchased by The Sultan of Brunei and his son Prince Jefri, who was on a bit of a spending spree. They bought the company and decided that they were going to sponsor Ferrari, because he likes Ferraris. He paid $50 million over three years, which was a crazy deal, to sponsor the team and then they had a £2 million budget to go and activate it. So it quickly became the number one invitation of the season, the one from Edward Asprey, to go to a Formula 1 Grand Prix.

I was busy entertaining these guests and we ended up flying around to ten meetings a year and I was only 26 years-old so I was flirting with all the wives, working with Michael Schumacher and Eddie Irvine and having a lot of fun!

At the same time I had just started working with an energy drinks company from Australia after running into a guy I played tennis with at the Vanderbilt Tennis Club, which was where Princess Diana and a lot of very well known people used to play, but is now a Westfield Shopping Centre. He said, "we've just started an energy drinks company, can you help us?" And I said, "er, yeah, sure!". He asked if I knew how to get distribution in Hungary and I said, "Yes, absolutely!", when of course I didn't know any distributors in Hungary. But it didn't take long to find one. The company was Hype Energy and their logos are all over the Benetton and Williams Formula 1 cars of the late 90s. It ended up that I was doing two jobs at once, with Hype Energy being the day job and Asprey the weekend one.

At the end of that period, both companies needed to go back to the Monaco Grand Prix and manage things, so I was booking rooms and tables and organising lots of things. Eventually we got to the point where I had created the yacht party with Asprey in '98 or '99, on a yacht called 'Iroquois' which is owned by a guy called John Henry who is a formidable entrepreneur and owns a hedge fund and some sports teams including the Boston Red Sox. Everyone thought the party was really great and it came about because we had been invited to go on the Ferrari yacht and we thought, well that's a good place to go, we'll take all our VIPs there, but the problem was that Ferrari's other sponsors were companies like FedEx, Panasonic, Shell and of course Marlboro. This meant that other visitors to that yacht were not the kind of people that would spend hundreds of thousands on a piece of jewellery - they were more likely to nick them! So I started my own little party for high net worth individuals in 2004 as a sort of charity event along with a brand partner that I was working with in Los Angeles and by then I had moved to LA because I'd started a beverage company and had also started working with a sponsorship agency and I was also representing the British Academy 'BAFTA LA' for sponsorship.

I arranged a deal with a company called Bombardier Business Aircraft because they said they'd like to do something in Monaco for clients, so I started an event that they sponsored and invited a whole bunch of my friends, because I'd been going to Monaco Grand Prix every year for ten years. So that's how it started in the beginning.

I then had discussions in LA with American Express who wanted to get involved, and this and that so I soon thought that I could start my own thing, which I called 'My Yacht Monaco'. When you go to the Monaco GP, you've got the opportunity to be in a grandstand or be in The Paddock Club, or some other boring environment, or you could be on a superyacht! And of course most people want to be on a superyacht. If you got an invitation that said, 'Would you like to come and sit on my terrace on Sunday afternoon to watch the Grand Prix?' but then another guy asks you to come to 'My Yacht Monaco', where are you going to go? You're going on the yacht every time!

It sounds like you had a combination of a 'he who dares' mentality when you spotted an opportunity that presented itself, and going 'balls out' to make something happen - does that sound like a fair observation?

Yes, it is a bit of a 'Who dares wins' situation and I think as an entrepreneur you have to do that. If you look at Richard Branson for example, he was making phone calls to get advertising for his student newspaper out of phone boxes and just trying the best he could. You need to do the best you can with what you have and you can't be intimidated by the system, because all of these 'Titans of Industry' started at the bottom somewhere and many of them have become very wealthy, some of them are completely full of themselves and very aloof, but there's also plenty of them who want to give back and want to help and are down to earth and humble. Those are the people that you need to try and reach out to, always try and reach for the top executives because everyone else is going to try and get in your way as they'll be thinking, "What's in it for me?", "What's my exposure?" and "How do I keep my job?" That last one is always the main thing that anyone thinks about, which is fair enough, they've all got mortgages and bills to pay, but it does mean that they may not necessarily want to help you.

I've always been a connector and it reminds me of a gentleman in Melbourne, Australia back in '96, and I met him when I stayed at his house actually. His name is 'Captain' Peter Janson, he's the Social Ambassador of Melbourne and he's a huge, huge character. We were in The Paddock Club in Melbourne and we were with all these VIPs and I was just doing my usual thing, I was walking around, chitty-chattying, socialising, flirting and making jokes, giving advice and my thoughts about Formula 1 and what's happening, taking people into the pit lane and introducing them to Michael Schumacher, etc. Janson came up to me and he said, "I've just been watching you for the last 20 minutes, and I thought I knew how to work a room, but I've never seen anyone work a room the way you do - and you're 26 years old!" This guy, in his role, is not exactly a wallflower either and I'd not really ever considered it before because for me it was just fun, I really enjoy connecting with people and introducing people.

I've always played that role, but the challenge of course is monetising it - how do you monetise connecting people? Everybody wants to meet other interesting people and do business deals, but you have to try and create a structure and a process, otherwise you'll get, "Thanks very much, I must buy you a drink." So that's where the My Yacht thing became an opportunity, to formalise things, because I ended up with a lot of friends that all wanted to go to the Monaco GP and would always ask me to arrange things for them and book hotels for them, etc., and I was like an unpaid concierge whose phone was ringing all the time. I was just doing it to try and help people. In creating the My Yacht business I could then say OK, here are the details, here's the yacht, this is the programme, it's super-premium, like-minded individuals and equally successful people - a lot of Ferrari owners, etc., and if you want to do it right, this is the way to do it.

Then slowly, after we did My Yacht Monaco for a few years, where I was travelling a lot, living between Monaco and the states and doing work for US companies, people started saying that my events are so good, with such a great atmosphere - which I didn't really realise, people just kept telling me this, but who was I to know if they're good or bad? Based on this feedback I decided I'd try to run an event at another place where that similar concentration of ultra-high-net-worth individuals is, so then we did Art Basel and Cannes Film Festival, which led to creating My Yacht Group - connecting the world's most interesting people in this multitude of hotspots around the world.

I'm sitting here in St Barths which is one of the epicentres of affluence, high society and glamour. It's the Monte Carlo of the Caribbean. I'm here because I ended up starting a yacht club here too, so all of these things just keep rolling into other things.

When you made that decision to set up My Yacht Monaco initially, how did you get started? What were the first things you put in place?

At the time I was working with the sponsorship companies and instead of making a 10 or 20 per cent cut on a deal I thought that if I owned my own brand then I could sell that and make more money and also own something which is valuable, rather than always selling someone else's 'real estate'. So setting up my personal brand was the first thing that I did.

When the idea came to you and you told family and friends what you wanted to do, what was their initial reaction?

In fact the beverage company was more of a challenge. Setting up Fuze Beverages with two partners, who were both older than me, twice my age in fact and more experienced in business. But again, I had already developed a better network of people, so I went out and ran around and ended up raising more than a million pounds, back in '97, out of some private investors to help fund the development of a new water beverage. It was water with added herbs and vitamins. I'm not a beverage specialist, but I am great at networking and great at selling and when I was hired by Hype Energy, they paid me £15,000 to go to Hungary and go and get some distribution deals. I had three or four friends in Hungary that I called up and I said, "Guys, I need to find distributors," and thankfully they knew some people that I could try speaking to. So I flew to Hungary and I got to work telling these people that this is 'the best thing since sliced bread', it's an energy drink, and literally they asked me, "What's an energy drink?" because nobody knew what it was in the early days of that market sector. I ended up with a guy called Yuval who was keen to be involved and said that he'd take the distribution for Hungary, Czech and Israel, so I ended up signing a deal with him some weeks later and it was the first big distribution deal that the company did.

They were obviously very pleased and said I was an absolute rock star and went on to say that they next wanted to get Asian distribution and who did I know in Hong Kong? At the time, in '97, I had to look in the Encyclopedia Britannica to find out where the hell Hong Kong was! I found it on the map, and it's quite a small place to find actually, and started thinking who on earth did I know in Hong Kong? Then I remembered that I'd met this one guy who I'd been skiing with a few years previously who lived there, so I called him up and he said that I should talk to a guy called Paul Chow because he knew everyone in Hong Kong. So next I called him to explain what I was doing and that I'd been told he might be able to help me, which he agreed he would and I told him that I'd be staying at the Mandarin Oriental - another very nice hotel. He was a young guy and he showed up in a Bentley, so I obviously thought, "Jesus, he's done well for himself", and he tried to make some introductions for me, which was very kind.

But actually I had more luck going into the minibar in my hotel room, pulling out all of the drinks, including all sorts of Asian ones that I wasn't familiar with, and seeing that on the back of the labels were the details of the local distributors. So I lined up all the drinks on my desk and just called up all these companies and said that I'm here with the world's number one energy drink company, who are involved with Formula 1, and I need to come and meet you. They agreed and I had my samples in my display case, which I'd kept cool in the minibar fridge, then sealed them into a cooler bag and jumped in a taxi to go over there. That went on for about a year and a half, whilst also working for Asprey and Ferrari, and from Hong Kong I went over to Kuala Lumpur where I was talking to Bacardi Martini and then Asahi in Tokyo, then down to Australia talking to Carlton & United Beverages and did all these deals. I came back with a 1.5 or 2 million case deal, which is enormous and they all thought I was a hero! I would earn 10c a case, so it was beginning to be a very profitable enterprise, up until the point where the founders, who were busy splurging the money on all sorts of fun times in Ibiza, fell out with the investors. This meant that unfortunately the wheels came off.

That's what started me in the whole drinks game as I understood the profitability potential of drinks so that's why we started our own little drinks company with the water herbs and vitamins, which was way ahead of its time back then.

People in the UK basically said, "What the fuck are you talking about?! Why do I need this?" I'd explain that it's very good for you, it's a natural energy water, it even has PMS helping properties for women, this one has got the equivalent of a liquid viagra in it and this one is great for hangovers. And they worked, we had four different variants, we signed up a London distributor and launched there and ran promotions at various nightclubs and things like that, and people liked it. We soon realised that there were bigger markets so I went trotting around Europe and I remember going to Hamburg and meeting the guys at Schweppes. They said that it really delivers and looks amazing, but they would have to do some research and testing which would take 6 to 12 months, and then do an analysis and then a small test run in a local market in the middle of Germany. I said that it's not going to work somewhere in the middle of Germany, you need to do it in a central city hub like Munich or Frankfurt. They said that this was the traditional process and the way that we do things so I was like "Fuck this, it's never going to work!" and we decided we'd head to the states instead.

One of my partners went over to Texas and I went out to California and started selling it on the beach. We'd shipped out sample cases because we found a bottling plant in Canada that would produce it for us, this was in Calgary, which was ironic because that's where I went bobsledding previously.

When I was selling it on Santa Monica Boulevard, Arnold Schwarzenegger was one of my first customers. He turned up in his Humvee and I said, "Mr. Schwarzenegger, hi, I'm Nicholas, and I wanted to show you this beverage. It's really good for you, and you should use it". And he said, "Ah, this is fantastic," and I said, "Can I have a picture?" He said, "Yah, of course!" So, we took a picture and I still have the photographs of him with his Humvee, and his kids getting out, and I gave him a couple of bottles. That was the difference when you got to California, but it's not so prevalent now unfortunately, the entrepreneurial atmosphere in the US has changed for the worse, in the last 15 or 20 years. But I remember at the time, it was just a very 'can do' environment. The UK and Europe, largely, was very much sort of "Why should I help you?", "It's not going to work", "Off you go with your silly little dreams again." Why is that? Why is it that Europe doesn't have a Silicon Valley? I mean, why the fuck? Why does everybody have to go to San Jose, California, if they have a good idea about technology?

The stuff that you do when you're young, it does have longevity, I'm not saying that you have to go to the Olympics, because it is not an easy thing to do, but you can do stuff which sets you up and gives you some credibility to help you get going to pursue your career, wherever that takes you. Life as an entrepreneur is like the Monte Carlo Rally up in the mountains above Monaco, which is full of twists and turns and bends and jumps, and accidents and you're going to have a lot of those, and you're going to get a lot more 'no's' than you get 'yes's'. And luck is a large part of it too, but I think what I have been very good at in my career is spotting the luck. Looking at opportunities, developing opportunities and being creative in thinking which adds value. So when you engage with people and you meet them, they could be very powerful, very wealthy and very good at a certain thing - but they won't necessarily have the same skill set that I have. And they are smart, so they're going to recognise that and so they might say, "Nicholas, you're like a marketing guru, I really want your help on this." And I'm like, "You want my help? You, a $100 million guy, want my help?!" They say, "Yeah, what do you think about this? You know a lot of people, you go around the world a lot more than I do." So if you can add value you become valuable - read up about things, be knowledgeable, be curious. I think it's really important.

What would you say was the hardest part of setting the My Yacht Group business up?

The hardest part is that it's all about marketing. It's sales and marketing. It's driving revenues. We all know that spending money is easy - setting up offices and spending money and buying photocopy machines, etc., that's easy. I've always been a firm believer of 'bootstrapping'. I'm a small-time entrepreneur compared to some of these guys who say that they're going to penetrate a trillion dollar industry, and they're going to try and get 5 per cent of it, and are going to raise $100 million. Personally, I'm not going to do that, it has never been my style. I've worked with people like that, and I take my hat off to them, but it's just not my style. It's not what I do. For me, it's all about bootstrapping, because every dollar out is another dollar you have to bring in.

Interestingly, you're going to have a lot of problems getting $100,000, because people don't want to invest $100,000, if you tell them it's $100 million, you're actually going to have more chance because the same process of due diligence and business plan reading and everything else happens, but it's just too small for a lot of investors. In that position you're going to have to go to guys who are your mates and see if they want to give you ten grand.

Were there any moments in setting up My Yacht Group when you thought you may have made a mistake? And maybe you shouldn't be doing it? Or was it just so obvious and the writing's on the wall that this would be used by people?

No, it's never obvious, you're always selling, you're always looking for opportunities. Our revenues are based on individuals and brands, so if I'm engaged with brands who don't want to do things, or don't have the budget then it's tough. You've actually got two types of brands, you've got ones who have vision and no budget, and ones with no vision and lots of budget. It's rare that you find one who's got both. Most marketing executives are not particularly visionary, because if they were they would be entrepreneurs themselves and not corporate executives.

To put on an event obviously costs a lot of money to make it happen.

How long did it take until you could make your first bit of money from that? Was it the first event or did you have to run a few to be able to take something from the business?

We've always been profitable. We've never lost money on an event. People had said to me, "Well, when you start this up, you're going to have to invest in the first year and you're gonna have to lose a couple of hundred grand," and I'm like, "You must be joking! I'm not losing a couple of hundred grand - I can't afford that!" I said we're just going to have to do it differently. Do it right. If we were going to lose money in an event, we just wouldn't do it. I don't commit to the events until we have a brand on board, because it's sponsor-led. If we have a brand that says that they've got a £50,000 budget, and they want to do this and want to do that, then we say great, and we do the event. Here's a list of opportunities that we can do and are appealing to, where would you like to do them geographically? And then we just go from there.

Did you run this yourself to start with or did you have a co-founder?

I still run it myself, of course, but I started it with my sister. I have to make mention of my sister, Annabel Frankel, my twin sister, because without her we wouldn't be halfway to where we are today. She's extremely efficient and does the job of about four people and she knows how to get stuff done and get organised. There's a lot of logistics involved in these types of events, a lot of moving parts.

We imagine the COVID-19 impact has rather slowed things down in terms of physical events, so it may well answer this question, which is what's been the hardest year so far? And what's been the best year?

In 2020 we didn't do any yacht events. We've done private dinners, where we moved the model on to private invitation-only, ultra high net worth dinners, which we have successfully done more than half a dozen of in 2020. And we're going to do some more here in St. Barts. And I think that just demonstrates the power and credibility of our network that we don't have to do an event on a yacht to get the right people to show up. I can actually reach out to people one-on-one and say, "I'd like you to come to a dinner and learn about going to space." Which is very exciting, but it's not relevant to everybody.

How do you manage your time? Do you have an assistant or anything like that?

No, I just wake up and get going. Every day.

Are you an early riser - up at 5am for a bit of fitness, perhaps?

No, I tend to work late at night, because there's less distractions, less phone calls, less interruption. Then I need to get seven or eight hours of sleep every night like everybody else, I think it's healthy. Then you wake up and you get going again. You've got to be self motivated. You've got to be a self starter. For a lot of people in these pandemic times, it's been very challenging to work in isolation, but thankfully I have not had any problems with that. Because I work in isolation all the time anyway, I'm always on my laptop, and I'm usually running around the world, talking to a world of relationships.

What would you say, are the three most important qualities that an entrepreneur should have? If you can think of three?

Well, look, the first thing is, you've got to pay your bills, right? Everything else sounds great - until you can't pay your electricity bill. So, if you have to live at home with your folks and start a business on your laptop in your bedroom, then that's what you have to do - and that's what many people have done. And today, we've got access to all of the resources. I mean, literally at your fingertips. Plus, you can use all these databases and social media networks and all these other things, to find people who otherwise were very difficult to find. So on the basis that you've got some shelter and you've got electricity, you know, the lights are on - although, let's remember that Mozart wrote quite nice music with candlelight.

Do you have a favourite famous quote, or one that you've heard from other entrepreneurs or successful people?

I used to have two mottos on my desk, one of them was 'Fear God, Dread Nought' - that's where the Dreadnought Battleships came from, back in the 19th century. And the other one said 'Enjoy life, this is not a dress rehearsal'.

2020 has probably cemented that more than anything. We all of course aspire to succeed, and I guess it depends upon what your definition of success is. And I would say that having a healthy family is important, having a good relationship with your children and your parents is vital. And no amount of money is going to provide that for you. At the end of the day, entrepreneurs are driven by a number of reasons, they are solitary in some respects, they go against the crowd. They are visionaries, they are creative people. But of course, they're also seeking the entrepreneurial success, depending upon what the definition is. I guess, by some terms, people might look at my career and say, 'he's very successful'. And I can look at my situation and say, "Well, if I'd only done this, this and this, I would have had more success." But what does that mean? A bigger company or more people involved, or a bigger brand... We've been approached now to sell the brand, so I guess, when you've got to a point where you have other entrepreneurs who look at your business, your revenues and the quality of your brand and make you offers of millions of dollars, then I guess you have to come to some conclusion that you've done something right. Because otherwise there wouldn't be a value in it, and you wouldn't have other intelligent people wanting to acquire your work for the last 15 years. So we've had those offers, and we continue to have those offers, and we are a very unique company. But if you look at it in terms of success, then for me it's having a wonderful group of friends around the world who trust you, and you get to spend time with and having an amazing lifestyle, which I do, and I'm very fortunate to be able to. But of course, to do that takes work, and it takes money. It also takes generosity from other people, because sometimes you're hosting them and sometimes they're hosting you. When you're standing on the quayside in Monaco, looking at a $50 million yacht and looking at the people on board, and either aspiring to be them or be like them, and assuming that because they're on the superyacht, and because they're wearing expensive watches and jewellery or whatever it is, that, therefore, they must be happier, they have to be happier than I am, right? It's just simply not true. Because all of these people have the same problems and the other stuff is just 'trimmings'.

What was the first luxury thing you treated yourself to in celebration of some early success? Are you a car man, was it an incredible watch, was it a home?

I've always invested my money in real estate - I don't spend it on this frivolous crap. I'm also very lucky because I was always working with luxury brands, so I've never had to actually buy a watch. Because I've always been given watches and things.

Cars are obviously a passion in my life, I've grown up around cars. I always said when I was 18 that I wanted to have a Ferrari by the time I was 25, and I could have had it then, but my father already had Ferraris, so I got to drive his and actually didn't have to. I was going on car rallies with rich people in the Gumball. I did the first Gumball Rally in '99 actually, and I had some money, but I didn't have the money that some of these guys had. They were driving brand new Ferraris, and I was thinking, "What the fuck do these guys do for a living?" They were all in real estate. In the first Gumball I drove a V8 Marcos Mantis, which was a very cool car and sounded amazing. But because I was working in the media and I knew all the PR companies and the car companies, they all used to send me cars anyway. It's much better to take someone else's car on a car rally rather than take your own, as long as you don't trash it.

I have an Aston which I bought years ago, which of course depreciated like a rock, a V12, but my pride and joy is a Ferrari F355 GTS six-speed manual, which I did buy after the Austin Grand Prix, where I set up a nightclub called 'My Yacht Club', when again, I'd never been a nightclub entrepreneur. I knew how to throw parties, and I had a brand and we hired a PR company, so we did a lot of stuff there. We made a lot of money that year, I mean, we made a lot of money in one weekend, and it was the easiest money I've ever made. It was hundreds of thousands and I just thought, "Wow! This is amazing!" and it was, it was fun. So I bought a 355 Ferrari at the low end of the market. I'd always loved that car and I was looking for a car for probably a year and a half. For me, it just encapsulates everything that's right about that period of time; engineering, performance, the lightness of the car, the way the car drives and handles, the engagement. I didn't get a red one though, I went with 'Titanium Grigio', which is a beautiful colour.

What does the next five years look like for you?

The next five years obviously depend on how we go with this COVID stuff, but I'm working a lot with different brands on consulting. We're doing a lot of behind the scenes consulting work, lining up lunches, deals and introductions, then we can have a signature event at some of the big destinations. We're going big at the Monaco GP next year and I'm very positive it's going to happen and then we'll do other activities.

People often ask me, what the next big thing is as we're always looking for opportunities. I'm on countless advisory boards of technology companies, medical device companies, I have a lot of contacts and relationships that I bring to these companies. So, I'm probably expanding that part of my life, continuing the events - we may end up selling the company to a bigger events company or an advertising agency, we've had some interest from some big names to be an ultra high net worth luxury brand event bolt-on to their existing business. Because not many people can really do what we do and have the access that we have.

I will always keep going, just keep plugging away.

NICHOLAS FRANKL

Instagram: @hun007 and @myyachtgroup

LinkedIn: https://www.linkedin.com/in/nicholasfrankl/

To help you get your business off the ground, or to a higher plane, we've brought together some of the finest minds from our own network to provide some succinct advice in their fields of expertise.

KEY TIPS FROM A CYBER SECURITY EXPERT TO KEEP YOU AND YOUR BUSINESS SAFE ONLINE

JAKE MOORE

Jake Moore is a Cyber Security Specialist at ESET, Europe's number one Internet Security and Antivirus company. He is also a well-respected industry expert who regularly provides commentary on a range of cyber stories in publications such as The Guardian, The BBC, The Independent and Forbes.

Starting a business is a very exciting time, the thrill of creating your website, the time spent organising your social media to look exactly the way you've always dreamed of and then finally the glory in making that first sale to your first customer. All of this is not only exciting, it is profitable which makes all those late nights and your hard work pay off. But what if your website got hacked? What if you couldn't access all of your files, your client database or worse still, lost all your hard-earned cash?

Although cyber security might not be on the forefront of your mind when you start a business, it is as important as your mission statement. Without protecting your intellectual property, you may as well throw caution to the wind and hope for the best. Sure, you may be ok but with daily cyberattacks taking down businesses every single day all around you but trust me, it is not worth the risk.

I investigated computer crime for over a decade for the police in the

Digital Forensics Unit and Cyber Crime Unit so I learnt a few tricks of the trade in how cybercriminals operate. I now work for an internet security company called ESET and my job is to make businesses of all sizes around the UK more secure, but above all, understand the risks.

Cyber security is like having car insurance. Without it, your car will still drive, get you from A to B as planned and even look quite cool in the process. But if something goes wrong, you could potentially walk away with nothing - and that's if you're lucky.

Protection in place doesn't have to be expensive nor time consuming, it just needs to be in place and made sure you are on top of it. I have met small businesses with under ten employees who are better equipped with their cyber security policies than some huge well-known international companies just waiting for the next big hack to make the front pages. It doesn't matter what size you are, cybercriminals are lurking in the deepest darkest depths of the internet taking aim on any business or email address they can locate.

So how can you protect your new company?

Ransomware

Ransomware is a type of malware that usually finds its way into your network via an email. Targeted or not, there will be an attachment included and some forceful wording to entice you to install the attachment. Once this occurs, every single file will be locked and that includes every file on the network including USBs plugged in and any other machines your device talks to. If your back up is incorrectly stored or even gets located by the malware, this could be game over for your business.

The hackers will then place a ransom note on your screen requesting money in a cryptocurrency (to avoid detection) to release the decryption key in order to get back up and running once again.

This can occur in any size business and in 2020 alone it happened to huge businesses such as Travelex, Garmin and Canon with some huge ransoms (up to $10million to release the data). The saddest part of all was that the ransoms were far higher than the cost of prior protection.

Backing up your data offline is the most important part of the business. Discover what your company could not survive without and make sure that is copied somewhere daily and not left plugged in to your network anywhere. Then once this is arranged, you must test the restore process in case of an attack as this will make you realise any vulnerabilities in the process and make you sleep easier should the inevitable occur.

Password Management

To not have your personal information featured in a data breach of some description would be quite a feat to achieve with the amount of data hacks we now see. One of the biggest problems in online protection is the use of poor passwords. It is absolutely vital that you do not reuse your passwords but people's dog's names, partner's birthdays and football teams are not only overused, but they are easily guessable with a little help from social media.

When I was working at the police, I would often have a locked device where the defendant had gone "no comment" on offering up the passcode. Part of my job was to therefore attempt to hack into defendant's devices and I would start by looking up their social profile online which would usually give me all I needed to crack in. Coupled with a tool where I could load their most important dates, names, teams and other personal information into, I could usually crack a password in the same day (any longer and I would be upset with myself). If the police can do this simple hack rather modestly, criminals can do it even quicker!

The problem is, passwords are the bane of most people's online lives, but they aren't going away any time soon. But never fear, a solution is already available and I would not start a business without one. This is the perfect opportunity to download and start using a robust password manager to help generate and store all your unique passwords. Password managers are extremely helpful and efficient in the protection of all online accounts helping you move away from using the same one or two passwords for all accounts. This helps not having to remember the ridiculous number of passwords for accounts you probably own. Once generated, each password should only ever be used once and never shared.

Your website and email are the most important accounts you now own. The passwords on these should be at least 20 characters long, a mixture of upper and lower case letters, numbers and symbols and completely unique. Furthermore, your accounts will also require the addition of two factor authentication, 2FA, to ensure extra protection on these accounts to thwart the constant barrage of attacks they will have to withstand.

Two factor authentication can be found in the account settings of all good applications and is extremely simple to set up. It adds security by sending a one-time use code to your authenticator app or via SMS every time you log in on a new device. Therefore, even if an attacker has your password, they will not be able to access it without your mobile phone. Without such protection, you could easily lose control of your social media and this in turn would suggest to your clients that you don't take their data very seriously. For example, I have seen businesses ruined after their Twitter feed has been hacked with indecent pictures posted which has then been rather difficult to explain the next time they have asked their bank for a loan.

Public Wi-Fi

If you are starting a business, there is a good chance you will be working remotely a lot of the time. There may be times where you won't be able to find a good enough 4G signal to complete your work so it can be tempting to jump on a public Wi-Fi hot spot such as in a coffee shop or in a hotel or airport. However, this is where lurking cyber criminals test out their skills on unbeknownst victims and can cause all sorts of damage including loss of accounts, data and even cash. It is possible (and I've been on the courses so I know how it is easily done) to hack into a device when using an insecure Wi-Fi network so make sure you do not use them without understanding the risks. Never use public Wi-Fi without installing a Virtual Private Network, VPN, first and only type in sensitive data when you're on a secure network such as at home or in the office.

Auto updates

To make your life as easy as possible, I would suggest you make your online process as autonomous as you can. Auto updating your laptop, phone, browser, website etc will force some of the best up to date protection onto your machine without having to think. Too many of us ignore security fixes, thinking they're either not that important or we're too busy to update the software on our laptop or phone. Except, in most cases, those updates are the result of discovering vulnerabilities that could have real-world consequences for our personal and professional data.

Vigilance

Finally, your awareness of scams in the form of phishing emails, fraudulent text messages or even convincing phone calls will prevent most attacks. Simply being aware of such attack vectors will allow you to pause and reflect on what is possible. If you lose the control of your site or your data, you could potentially lose control of your business. Nowadays cyber insurance is on offer from all good insurers, but this is seen as a reactive reaction rather than proactive protection. Protecting your most valuable assets with the knowledge and awareness can be far cheaper in the long run and after it is set up correctly and with the right procedures in place, you will be able to focus more time back on the business and start making more money securely.

www.jakemoore.uk

Twitter: @Jake_MooreUK

KEY TIPS FROM AN ACCOUNTANT ON THE TYPES OF BUSINESS AND THE SUPPORT YOU MAY NEED

LUKE PIPER

At the age of 18 I didn't know much, but I did know that I was not going to go down the traditional route of University after finishing my A-Levels. I had only one plan, and that was to run a business. I didn't even know what sort of business, or have any real direction at the time, but I knew that was what I wanted to do.

So I applied for a job as an accountant and thinking back to the time this all happened, I remember clearly thinking, "what does an accountant do?" I went to my Dad and asked him that very question. All of my family are employed civil servants mainly in the healthcare profession, and I was the first to be talking about running a business. So my Dad's answer to my question was not one that came from any experience of ever dealing with an accountant, and it was along the lines of "I'm not too sure what they do, but they help businesses to work out money and figures". Well for me, that was enough to think it would be a good starting point to setting up my own business one day and thankfully I got the accountancy job.

Fast forward another 18 years and as irony would have it, accountancy ended up being the business that I now run and also my understanding of what accountants do is a bit more rounded than back then.

So what do accountants do?

There are two main roles: 'number crunching' and 'advisory'. Both are needed and crucial services for every business, but it is fair to say that as the world keeps evolving into the digital and real time era, number crunching is becoming less of value and advisory is becoming more valuable than ever before.

Number crunching is as the very name suggests, the collation and presentation of the figures that a business produces, and in most cases it will be all based on historical data. The numbers in a business are collated for three main parties; firstly, the owner of the business in order to understand if the company is making any profit – otherwise what's the point? Second is for the tax authorities in order to report and pay the taxes owed by the business – a necessary evil, and the third is for external parties such as banks and suppliers who will look at the figures in order to make decisions such as lending money, for example. Number crunching is crucial and essential, but it is not particularly exciting and although it's probably the main service offered by an accountant, it adds little forward benefit to a business owner. Some accountants rarely step foot outside of the number crunching space and therefore will only ever cover one of these two main services for a business.

Advisory services are all about adding value to a business using the accountant's knowledge, experience, and the business data in order to offer strategic and profitable advice. If you think about it, an accountant sees multiple different businesses every day, ones that fail and ones that succeed. They talk regularly to owners of businesses large and small and to other key third parties such as banks and other professionals. All of this and more shows the accountant as a very useful resource when key business decisions need to be made. The main barrier that most people have in accessing this resource though, is that accountants charge for their time, as there is nothing else for them to sell, and so 'a chat' often comes with a cost.

That being said though, for those clients that embrace the advisory capacity of their accountant, it can save unquantifiable amounts of time and money.

If you wanted to start in business tomorrow as a prime example, you have two main choices, either to register as a sole trader, or as a limited company. You can Google advice and try to understand the jargon and differing opinions and hopefully make a decision that is right for you, but then what about all of the paperwork and registrations needed? An accountant does this on a daily basis, and so paying for an hour of a qualified accountant's time (very important to use a *qualified* accountant by the way!) and get some bespoke advice about the right setup for you will save you one big headache. No size fits all, and where a limited company might be right for one, the same justification may not suit another.

So in order to decide the best accountant for you, I would recommend doing the following –

- Always speak to 2 or 3 accountants before appointing one to look after you and your business. It is a relationship that could last many years, and so it is important to get it right at the start.

- Speak to friends and family for any personal recommendations for accountants they use, as a recommendation goes a long way.

- Always, always, **always** use a qualified accountant. The differences and potential long term issues of not doing this vastly outweigh any cost savings that may be available from using 'my mate's friend from the pub'.

By doing the above it should increase the chances of picking an accountant that not only number crunches, but brings a lot more to the table for any aspiring business owner.

www.bkbaccountants.co.uk

KEY TIPS FROM A HEALTH AND FITNESS EXPERT ON LOOKING AFTER YOUR BODY AND MIND WHEN SETTING UP A BUSINESS

BEN HULME

Being entrepreneurial myself I quickly learned that health is our most valuable commodity. More so than money. You can always get more money, but once your health deteriorates it's very hard to get it back. As you will discover, I learnt this the hard way.

Don't become a workaholic. Some time away from your business is important for your brain and your body. I recommend that you start by dedicating just one hour a day to becoming the best version of you. You won't regret it, plus you'll still have 23 hours to do whatever else you need to do.

This hour to yourself won't be wasted. For example you could go for a walk whilst listening to personal development podcasts, so that you're exercising your body and your mind at the same time. Lack of time is not an excuse. For example, if you watch Netflix (like most people) you could invest in a spin bike and cycle in front of your TV instead of just sitting on the couch when you have some down time. L.I.S.S (Low Intensity Steady State) cardio is a fantastic calorie burner and will help you to get healthier without changing your lifestyle too much. You could do home workouts like the ones I have for you at BootCampVault.com This means you don't have to spend time travelling to and from the gym. These workouts torch body fat and help you to get in epic shape fast, no matter what your current fitness level is.

It's important to remember that you can't out train a bad diet though, so let's start with some quick pointers about nutrition. The most important thing is hydration. You need to drink two to three litres of water per day - and this doesn't include coffee! Obviously food is your primary energy source but it's more complex than that because it can also cause your energy levels to crash and that all comes down to a delicate balance between what you are consuming and your hormones.

In simple terms, carbs are your main energy source. If you are eating the wrong carbs at the wrong times, you are going to spike your insulin and then your energy levels will crash, making you less productive. I highly recommend that you focus on consuming unrefined/complex carbs rather than refined/simple carbs and try to consume your carbs earlier in the day and less in the evening before you rest (unless you are exercising at night). I recommend three meals a day so you can live a relatively normal lifestyle but also healthy snacks between meals so your body is constantly burning food which will ultimately speed up your metabolism.

If you don't have much time to prepare fresh food then prepare beforehand so that you are less likely to grab unhealthy snacks throughout the day. Avoid processed and ultra-processed foods and focus on the types of food that were available a few thousand years ago, because that is what we are designed to eat. Lots of the modern food that we buy is full of all sorts of nasties such as artificial sugars, salt and preservatives, which directly have an impact on our health. So focus on going back to basics a bit, have the fruit, the vegetables and the good quality protein but avoid the 'grab and go' food that we have all got so used to.

So how do I know this stuff? Well, I run a successful fitness business with a boot camp, an online health and fitness platform and I have written two books myself (one on nutrition and mindset and the other on personal development for success). I have helped thousands of people to achieve success with their health and fitness efforts. But it wasn't always like this for me.

At 24 years old I was the passenger in a Lamborghini when the driver lost control (at speed) and hit a tree. I ended up breaking my neck and having to go through a huge operation to save my life. I am grateful every day for the fact that I am not paralysed and still here to share my story with others.

Due to the nature of the accident I developed PTSD and I got myself into a rut of obesity, anxiety and depression. It was a scary time and instead of focusing on my health, I channelled all my energy into something I felt I could control - my business. However, I used my injury and the fact that I was busy with my startup business as an excuse not to exercise or to eat healthily. I turned to junk food and takeaways as comfort (and convenience) and that compounded into a really unhealthy, overweight and depressed version of me. I ended up on antidepressants and I desperately needed to sort myself out, but I was in a spiral.

One day my whole world changed when my relationship broke down. I became a full time single Dad to my daughters and I had to focus on them. I had to close my business and totally change my lifestyle due to my commitments to my kids. Focusing on health and fitness genuinely saved my life and it made me a better father and businessman too. To put things into context, I ended up losing 5.7 stone and transforming my body, I came off my antidepressants and totally changed my mindset. Now I have helped thousands of people thanks to my story and the business that I have created and I really hope that I can help you on your journey to success in all aspects of your life.

For my books, home workouts and much more check out my links here: Linktr.ee/benhulme

I am here to help, so feel free to reach out via my socials @BootCamperFitness

Become the best version of you, you won't regret it.

Ben Hulme
AKA The Boot Camper

THE VANTAGE
NETWORK VIEW

We have thoroughly enjoyed meeting all of the amazing entrepreneurs in this book and have learnt so much from them along the way. Here are some observations that we have made, distilled into a few points to help you.

1. Perseverance is key. Every entrepreneur hits many low points on the rollercoaster, but your mindset is one of the few things that you have complete control over, and the most successful people on the planet all have such a strong belief that they would make their ideas a success.

2. Reach out and speak with people. There certainly is a lot to be said for the old adage 'It's all about who you know'. If you reach out to the right people, whether you know them or not, then you shouldn't be scared that they might steal your incredible idea - a true entrepreneur loves to help another out if they can.

3. Keep things simple. It's tempting to go nuts and try to do everything at once, particularly when you're brimming with excitement and impatient to get your product or service out there. However, everyone that features in this book has said the same thing - take things one step at a time and try to work smarter, not harder - particularly if you are doing something as a side hustle.

4. Celebrate the small wins! It's so easy to only notice the little milestones and achievements when looking back, so take a moment to crack open a bottle of fizz when you launch, when you sell your first contract, when you hit 1,000 subscribers, etc. You deserve it.

5. You don't have to reinvent the wheel. Find something that you are either passionate about and can monetise, or something that solves a problem. You don't need to waste time trying to come up with something that nobody has ever done before, the chances are that most things have already been done to a level, and if it hasn't, there's probably a reason why. Find something that you make unique, do in a different way or package/ sell in a different way and then it comes down to putting it in motion.

We would love to hear from you!

Email us at info@vantage-network.com or send us a DM on social channels @vantagenetwork.

Thank you again for reading this.

Ben and Henry.

THANK YOU

Melanie Faldo
Red Carpet Communications Ltd
redcarpetcomms@gmail.com
https://www.linkedin.com/in/melanie-faldo

James W Phillips
https://jwpmediagroup.com
https://www.linkedin.com/in/james-w-phillips-3794a7ab/

Rosie Whitelock at Bonacia Ltd - a brilliant publisher that
understands startups and entrepreneurs.
https://bonacia.co.uk